G000079046

UNDERGROUND, OVERGROUND

OVERGROUND

The fault lines of football clubs

Andi Thomas

HALCYON
PUBLISHING

Published by Halcyon Publishing

First published 2021

Edited by Adam Bushby & Rob MacDonald

ISBN: 978-1-9196240-1-3

Cover design: Peter Rowson
Layout: Rob MacDonald

Printed & bound by:
Bell & Bain Ltd
303 Burnfield Road
Thornliebank
Glasgow
G46 7UQ

For Mike

Repetition. Repetition. Repetition.
David Peace

Contents

About the author

Andi Thomas has been writing about football since 2010, and has written for *SB Nation*, *ESPN*, *Eurosport*, *The Blizzard* and various other websites and publications. In 2012 he was named Blogger of the Year by the Football Supporters' Federation. He has co-authored two Premier League diaries, both available from Ockley Books. This is his first solo book. He lives in south London.

Acknowledgements

Thank you to Dr. Gavin Weston and Frédéric Carver.

Thank you to Mike Counsell, Juliet Jacques, Greg Johnson, Scott Oliver and Charlie Talbot.

Thank you to Adam and Rob at Halcyon.

Thank you to the Old King's Head and all who sail in her.

Thank you to everybody that answered my questions, filled out my surveys, lent me their thoughts, shared their work, wrote books that I borrowed things from, helped me dig out documents, and listened tolerantly and with great patience as I worked all of this out.

Thank you to Trudy. Thank you to Rosa.

Introduction

What is a football club?

This is an easy question with an obvious answer. If you're reading this, chances are you have a favourite one. Perhaps you go to their ground every week or so and watch them play; perhaps you do so occasionally, or not at all. But even if you don't have a club to call your own, you'll know that a football club is, roughly speaking, a group of people that work together to make a football match happen by providing one of the two teams required. Small, amateur clubs do so for the pleasures of their members; large, professional ones sell t-shirts.

The easy answer is no doubt fine, as far as it goes, but in a very important sense it fails to go far enough. Leaving aside the amateur clubs: why, if this is all that football clubs are, are they supported? Why are they supported in such grand and overwhelming ways? 'You'll Never Walk Alone' has accompanied couples down the aisle and coffins into the flames. Children are named for footballers, arms are inked with badges, faces, trophies, important dates. Memories are tethered to footballing moments and lives are measured out against them. Football grounds shape and even dominate cities: the largest of them hunch against the urban skyline like cathedrals, floodlight-spires jagging into the air.

Perhaps we might think about other things that football clubs resemble, other institutions of social importance. Stare at any given football club for long enough and some familiar shapes will emerge. There's a bit of a parish church in there, and a bit of a community centre. There's a lifestyle brand, and a theatre for both pantomime and drama, and a museum, and a pub, and a social club and a reading group and a choir and a comedy improv troupe and an argument — lots of arguments — and maybe even a bit of a folk tale as well. History, society and culture, comedy and tragedy. All stitched together into this strange chimera: a football club. And, of course, while all football clubs are fundamentally quite similar, each football club is distinct from every other in important and particular ways, like a large and uncommonly exciting bag of Revels.

Another question. Who do football clubs belong to? When it comes to professional clubs, the legal entities belong to whoever has shelled out the money that the last owner was looking for, be that Roman Abramovich or Mike Ashley, the City Football Group or Manchester United plc. But this is an uncomfortably technical answer, correct and dispiriting: we can counter by suggesting that they also belong, in a far more powerful sense that probably wouldn't stand up in court, to their fans.

In the early years of the 21st century, something highly unusual happened to one of England's football clubs. The owners of south London club Wimbledon FC were given permission to move the club some sixty-odd miles north, to the new town of Milton Keynes. For anybody unfamiliar with the story there will be more details later, but for now suffice it to say that this was exceptionally controversial. In response, and after their various protests had ultimately failed, a number of Wimbledon fans formed a new club, AFC Wimbledon.

Where once there had been one club, now there were two. One bore the name, the league position, and was essentially the same corporate and legal entity, just in a different place (although it wasn't too long before Wimbledon FC went bankrupt, entered administration and then re-emerged as MK Dons). Meanwhile, AFC were still located in south London, but had to play their games in a temporary home and were starting all over again as semi-professionals, near the bottom of English football's sprawling pyramid.

This book is about the consequences of that move. Not the practical consequences for Wimbledon or MK Dons, but the consequences for English football in general, and the questions that the move forced English football to ask itself. And this was, truly, a matter for English football as a whole: one of the more interesting features of the story is that it quickly went beyond those fans directly involved and became a national concern, a national argument.

When I first started thinking seriously about writing something related to Wimbledon, I began from the following sketched-out question.

> Isn't it strange that pretty much everybody that's interested in football, famously a game of opinions and frequently a game of extremely heated disagreements, agrees that what happened to Wimbledon was, in some sense, not right?

Obviously there are plenty of answers, caveats, counterpoints, and further questions to be asked from there — at the very least, "Pretty much everybody" is probably an overstatement — and you may even like to disagree with my entire premise. And that's fine. Say what you like about football, but having opinions is definitely a game of opinions. But after some refinement, I decided it would be reasonable to work outwards from three basic assumptions:

1. a significant number of football fans, perhaps even the majority, had and still have at least some problem with what happened to Wimbledon;
2. a significant number of that significant number were and are still actively appalled; and
3. neither 1 nor 2 applies to Wimbledon fans only.

Looking for an explanation to point 3 in particular, I realised that while what happened to Wimbledon was obviously extraordinary in its final outcome, the broad dynamics behind the split were familiar, perhaps even commonplace. At heart, this is a story of a club's owners messing around with a club to the great frustration and unhappiness of the fans, and that is a story that has been repeated over and over at every level of the game.

Newcastle United, Cardiff City, Hull City, Charlton Athletic, Blackpool, Manchester United, Dulwich Hamlet, Macclesfield Town, York City, Portsmouth ... the list goes on. In fact, it might be quicker to list those clubs whose fans have never been put through some manner of owner-instigated strife. As far as I can tell, that's none of them.

Generally, this messing around tends to manifest in less spectacular ways, such as poor transfer decisions or managerial appointments, or occasionally changes to kit colours or the club crest. And these are met with varying levels of anger in the stands, on phone-ins, and on social media: a full-scale relocation and subsequent phoenix club is extremely rare. But the idea of a divide between 'the club' — that is, the owner, the directors, the associated executives; the people who actually run the thing — and 'the fans' — which we can define broadly as people that are interested in a club but generally not practically involved with running it — is a persistent and widespread one. A frankly depressing survey carried out by the Football Supporters' Federation in 2017 found that 68% of English football fans felt that their club did not care about them or their views.

Wimbledon's split — or relocation, or death and rebirth — was a moment of existential crisis that brought this near-universal tension out into the light and forced Wimbledon's fans, and football fans in general, to confront and interrogate their own ideas of what a club is and is not, should and should not be. To consider what is critically important about a club's identity, what defines that identity, and what an appropriate response might be when this identity is threatened. Forming a new club is a step beyond simply ceasing support for your old one: were AFC's new fans abandoning their club, or had their club abandoned them? And beyond that question, a tangle of others, most notably: why, if you pick a football club up and put it down somewhere else, will the broad sweep of the football community respond by saying "Hang on, no, that's not right"?

To make it clear up front, while I am not a Wimbledon fan, I count myself among those that objected to the move at the time, and have continued to view it as a shabby business that should never have been permitted. But this book is not a history of the move, nor is it a polemic against it. Rather, it is a series of interconnected thoughts about the implications of the move, and of the actions of all those involved at the time and in the years since. It is also an exercise in opinion-taking: the book began its life as a dissertation for an MA in social anthropology, which I completed in September 2019, and as such it's not really about what I think at all. I asked a lot of football fans a lot of questions: about Wimbledon, about AFC and MK Dons, about the split, and matters arising. Questions of continuity and history, and who gets to define the first and lay claim to the second. And I asked everybody the question we began with: What is a football club?

The answers that football fans gave to that question, and what those answers might point towards, is what this book is really about. My fundamental thesis is that a football club's identity is made in large and ultimately overwhelming part by its fans. By its fans doing nothing more complicated than being fans, over and over again. My case for this begins with Wimbledon; my hope is that it ends up everywhere.

Including, and to start with, Newcastle. If you do as I did, and ask a lot of football fans to define what a football club is, you will find that a fair few of them are happy to pass the question on to English football's highest moral authority, the late Bobby Robson. The former Ipswich, England, Barcelona and Newcastle United manager came, by the end of his life, to occupy an unusual position within English football, as perhaps the only person of stature, achievement and wide-ranging influence that pretty much everybody liked. Accordingly, a number of my survey respondents were able to quote his famous definition of a football club in full, while others could just write "Sir Bobby's definition", or "What Bobby Robson said", and trust that I'd know what they meant. And they were right.

What is a club in any case? Not the buildings or the
directors or the people who are paid to represent it.
It's not the television contracts, get-out clauses, marketing
departments or executive boxes. It's the noise, the passion,
the feeling of belonging, the pride in your city. It's a small boy
clambering up stadium steps for the very first time, gripping
his father's hand, gawping at that hallowed stretch of turf
beneath and, without being able to do a thing about it, falling
in love.

The enduring appeal of this definition is not just down to Robson's
lovely turn of phrase. It is a definition in two competing parts, positive
and negative: not this or this but that and that. It is an argument.
It asserts the existence of that same fault line identified above, the
distinction between the club as a thing that is owned by a person
or a few people, often chaotically and sometimes destructively, and
the club as a thing that belongs to all its fans. Indeed, though he
wasn't talking about actual fan ownership, Robson's club is a thing
made both by and of fans: present and engaged, active and affected,
helplessly in love. To support a football club is an act of creation.

Robson's definition is particularly pointed when considered in
the context of Newcastle United. The book from which it is taken,
Newcastle – My Kind of Toon, was published in 2008, a few years
after Robson had been surprisingly and rather brutally sacked
as manager. At that time the club was under the control of the
widely unpopular Douglas Hall and Freddy Shepherd, who became
notorious when they were covertly recorded in a Spanish brothel
calling Geordie women "dogs" and mocking the cupidity of the
club's supporters. They eventually sold the club to Mike Ashley, the
London-based billionaire chief executive of Sports Direct, whose
stewardship of the club has descended into farcical tragicomedy.

The Ashley years have provided enough material for a book all its
own, but perhaps the most emblematic act of violence towards the
idea of Newcastle United came when Ashley briefly changed the name
of St James' Park, the club's home ground since their foundation in

1892, to 'sports-direct.com@St James' Park Stadium', @-sign and hyphen and all.[1]

Newcastle United's ownership travails may be unusually baroque, but the shape is that same familiar story: the club's owners, the club's fans, the agitation of the latter by the inadequacies of the former. And yet never at any point does the identity of the club become wholly subsumed by that person or regime. Mike Ashley is not and has never been definitive of Newcastle United; indeed, the more ridiculous his time in charge gets, the more he presents as some parasitic entity, attached but separate. This broad distinction between the two aspects of a football club is applicable to more or less any club going, as is the sense that fundamentally the club is not them, in there; it's us, out here.

By presenting his definition as an argument, Robson folds this sense of contestation into the very idea of the club itself: it is not just that the club is made up of the fans and their affection, but that it is so in the face of this other conception, this other idea of what a club might be. What it cannot be allowed to be. There is, too, a sense of time passing: hands held across generations, the club tended and bequeathed. It is a constant process of affection, made and made again. And it is, of course, universal: we know that Bobby Robson is talking about his city of Newcastle, his beloved Newcastle United, but his definition is generous enough to encompass the world. This falling in love may happen in one particular place — that intersection of

---

[1] At the time of writing, Ashley has recently failed to sell the club to the sovereign wealth fund of the Kingdom of Saudi Arabia, whose other ongoing interests include the macabre butchery of dissident journalists and a brutal war in Yemen. This failure has of course saved the club from the ignominy of becoming a sportswashing vehicle, though the Premier League's foot-dragging over the bid appears to have been inspired by television rights, not human rights. If there is a moral silver lining, it comes around a pungently amoral cloud, and as it stands the club's involvement in sportswashing will continue to be limited to two heavy defeats per season at the feet of Manchester City. Ashley, for his part, has railed against the "dark forces" preventing the club from becoming "the powerhouse that fans deserve", and is seeking arbitration.

young fan with steps, hand and turf — but the world is filled with such particular places. Every club has one. Many stories of football support begin with one.[2] To support a football club is to carry out a specific and localised version of a near-universal practice: clubs are necessarily distinct but they are also categorically alike, just as every love story is its own irreplicable variation on a common theme of shared intimacy, humanity and joy, as similar and as wholly individual as snowflakes.

The way in which Robson's definition has become a touchstone suggests that plenty of football fans want to think about their clubs in the same way he did his: as something made beyond the corporate boxes and panelled boardrooms. As hundreds and thousands of localised love stories; as the continual creation and re-creation of affection and devotion, renewed every time a fresh pair of wide eyes falls onto the same bounded green space.

---

[2] And many do not, of course: they begin through television or on the playground or down the park or through family ties or through any of the other hundreds of ways an impressionable child — or adult — might encounter and be enraptured by a football club. This is clearly an idealised sketch; however, it is a resonant one. Perhaps all football stories should begin this way. Or perhaps all football stories should feel as if they could have begun this way.

A note on method

Though this book has an academic origin story, in its fuller and expanded form it is certainly not a piece of academic writing. I am not even quite sure it is correct to describe it as a work of anthropology, at least not in a strict sense, even though there is some amount of method, theory and participant observation in here. But while I am happy to concede the noun, I will claim the adjective: I hope that I have written something *anthropological*.

There are as many competing definitions of what anthropology is as there are anthropologists to come up with them — another game of opinions — but Tim Ingold came up with my favourite when he wrote that anthropology is "philosophy with the people in". That is the spirit in which I have attempted to think about the subjects of this book, about football clubs and the practice of football support: as fundamentally peopled. I believe that the best way to think about something that people do is to think about how the people that do it, do it, even if that might lead to some awkwardly constructed sentences. And how they think about how they do it, and how they apply that thought, and on through time and habit and history.

Further, I would like to suggest that a lot of football writing is anthropological in spirit. The practical heart of anthropology is the business of researching and producing ethnography: the anthropologist goes to a place, watches the people of the place as they go about their ordinary business, and then writes it all up.[3] And football writing has often been produced with just this kind of people-watching spirit. I think of books like *The Bromley Boys* by Dave Roberts; *Family* and *The Nowhere Men* by Michael Calvin; *A Season with Verona* by Tim Parks; and of course Harry Pearson's wonderful meanders around football in the north-east of England, *The Far Corner* and *The Farther Corner*. And there are many more. If we were to try to parcel these off into genres other than 'football writing' we'd end up with journalism, travel writing, memoir, perhaps social history. None of them is an ethnography in the academic sense; none of them is trying to be. Yet they are all fundamentally ethnographic, fundamentally anthropological: they attend closely to the lives of football people as they are lived, and to the practice of being a football person as it is carried out.

A good chunk of the data underlying this book comes from a survey I carried out in late February and early March of 2018. I should make it clear that this survey was not designed to be representative of how the football-supporting population of England in general feels about any of the issues raised. The results have not been weighted for population, age, or any other demographic variation, and are almost certainly skewed in a number of exciting and peculiar directions. That's what happens when you collect data online.

---

[3] Done well, anthropology is a generous, modest, empathetic social science, one that engages honestly and openly with the strange and delightful notion that people are all the same and are all different, all at the same time. But the discipline is riddled with problematics, from the localised implications of the anthropologist, frequently a privileged outsider, inserting themselves into a community with the explicit intention of treating that community as an object of research, through to the deep entwinement of much of anthropology's past and present with colonial administrations and legacies. It has been called, not unfairly, a 'child of Western imperialism', and in one way or another has been reckoning with that ancestry ever since. I can recommend *Anthropological Controversies* by Gavin Weston and Natalie Djohari for a good historical overview of some of these issues. And I can hope that my own position as one of the fans I am talking about helps me to avoid some of the starker problems.

Accordingly, every mention of a percentage or a trend from this survey should be taken with a caveat: this is such-and-such percent of a highly unusual sample, comprising people who (a) use one or other social network in common with the author or with another person that shared the survey; (b) were online on or after February 28, 2018; and (c) were happy to fill in a survey that drifted across their news feed with a note reading 'REQUEST FOR HELP'. Such respondents cannot, I suspect, be added up and divided down into the average person on the Clapham Rovers terraces, and I do not claim them as such. What I was after, and what I received, was a rich seam of qualitative data from which I could think outwards.

There were two questions in the survey of particular importance. The first came in two parts, beginning with:

Which of these statements is closest to being true?

- AFC Wimbledon are a continuation of Wimbledon FC
- MK Dons are a continuation of Wimbledon FC
- neither AFC Wimbledon nor MK Dons are a continuation of Wimbledon FC

And continuing with:

If your first thought upon reading the question above was 'Well, it's far more complicated than that', could you explain why?

As indicated in the introduction, the second question was:

This question is deliberately vague — answer it in any way you like: What is a football club, really, when you get right down to it?

I will go into much more details about these questions in part three, but for now I will simply say that I was hoping to gather answers that, while certainly not rigorously or precisely representative, nevertheless pointed towards how some football fans might consider questions of club identity, continuity, and being. Ultimately I ended up with more than 1,000 responses to this question, most of them distinct and clearly heartfelt, some of them funny, and a few pleasantly obscene. These answers were not the end point but the start, to be read into and read outwards from. They have not dictated the contents of this book but they have informed every part of it. For ease of reference, whenever you see a floating quotation indented and italicised —

Like this.
And like this.

— then it is an answer from my survey, whether directly attributed or not.

Two further clarifications. First, the scope of this book is generally limited to English football, for reasons of time and personal capacity, though I hope it will be of interest beyond. And second, most of the contents of this book should apply as equally to women's football as to the men's game. Generally speaking this is not a book about the sport as it is played but as it is supported, and while football crowds remain male-dominated spaces, sometimes unpleasantly so, the on-field gender division in the professional game should be largely irrelevant. However, women's football in England has an unusual and controversial history: in 1921, the Football Association banned women's teams from using any ground affiliated to either the FA or the Football League. This ban lasted 50 years and had shattering consequences for women's football as an organised spectator sport. I consider this in more detail in chapter five.

And finally, a statement of intent. Or perhaps a statement of the lack of it. I do not intend this book to stand as a definitive statement of football's cosmology, or a universal declaration of the rights of fans, or anything so grand. Nor am I trying to explain why any person likes football; still less people in general. Football support is highly subjective and deeply personal, and I cannot hope and do not pretend to speak for everybody. I do not think any of my answers close off any of my questions; I do not particularly want them to. I offer this all lightly, in the hope that it is interesting. And while I do not necessarily prescribe this way of conceptualising the identity of a football club — a thing made of its fans, made by its fans, made for its fans — I am happy to say that, on balance, I recommend it.

PART ONE:
The wider interests of football

Chapter One:
Where do football clubs come from?

While the 2020/21 season will go down in footballing history as one of the strangest, there was little surprising about the eventual results. For the third time in four years, the humanitarian outreach project of St Mark's Anglican Church won the Premier League, and while the works team of the carriage and wagon department of the Lancashire and Yorkshire Railway came in second, it was a distant second. At the other end of the table, the footballing wing of Sheffield United Cricket Club were relegated early, and were soon joined by the company team of the Salter's Spring Works, West Bromwich and Fulham St Andrew's Church Sunday School FC. Meanwhile a splinter club from the Norwich Church of England Young Men's Society won the Championship and, well, you get the idea.

Other readings of the season are available. At the same time as all of the above was happening, the sovereign wealth fund of Abu Dhabi reclaimed the title from Fenway Sports Group and left NYSE: MANU as distant runners-up, while Roman Abramovich's pet football team took fourth place. I do not mean here to set these two readings against one another: to argue that the present moment amounts to a corruption or debasement of what came before. Organised football in England has always existed within and around organised capitalism in England, ever since it moved from the playing fields of the public schools to the heart of the industrialised cities, and that it should have become globalised alongside the economy is not a surprise, whatever one might think of the consequences.

But what is striking about that first account, and indeed about the broad mass of English football clubs in general, is that the vast majority have what we might loosely call 'community' origins. Church teams founded to do good work in their local area, works teams founded to fill the weekends and ward off the demon drink. Cricketers looking for something to do in the winter, old schoolboys looking for something to fill their adult lives. That is, they were founded by a particular group of people in a particular place, often connected to an organisation or collective already in existence, who one day decided that it would be a good idea to play football together. *Guardian* journalist Barney Ronay has suggested that since "these clubs existed as an extension of their local community," they serve as a "living riposte [to] the Thatcherite notion that there is no such thing as society".

Thinking about this as a process, there is an important early moment in the making of any football club. How and why, for example, did Newton Heath become Manchester United? That particular story involves the board of the Lancashire and Yorkshire Railway looking for something non-alcoholic for their employees to get up to, then an ambitious club president arranging games for the carriage works team against more distant and grander opponents. Some cup victories followed, then a gamble on two grandstands. As the club grew, it cut ties with the railroad company and then, in 1892, received an invitation into the expanding Football League. The name change came ten years later. But the most interesting moment among these developments is one common to all professional and semi-professional clubs: a simple, strange, quietly wonderful occurrence. People started going to watch them play.

England's professional football clubs emerged from a productive historical conjuncture around the end of the 19th century, as labour organisations carved a small space for living out of the working week. Saturday afternoons off, a little money to spend, rising literacy, and a relatively cheap rail network around much of the country: perfect conditions for the working classes to not only watch football games, but to follow football clubs that, by this point, were all playing the same game with the same rules. And so a tin passed around a crowd became a roll of tickets, then a turnstile; a rope around the pitch became a fence, then along came another fence to keep the unticketed out. Then came a stand on the halfway line, another opposite, one at each end if demand was high enough. The question of football fans is answered by the construction of a football ground: such a club, usually semi- or fully professional by this point, needs a place to live that goes beyond a pitch to play on. Clubs had to organise not just their players but their supporters. Organised football games quickly became not just things to be played but things to be watched.

This is, of course, a generalised picture painted in broad strokes. But I think it's fair to say that once a club begins to attract fans in significant numbers, those fans then become a significant part of what that club is. Fans may not be able to play in the games, but they do have certain advantages over the players when it comes to identification with a particular club, not least that a career as a fan can last much longer than a career as a player. Go to your first game aged ten or so, go to your last aged 80: that's a 70-year stretch. Not even Stanley Matthews lasted that long. And most players aren't at a single club their entire career; some don't even last a full season.

In *Games Without Frontiers*, the writer and critic Joe Kennedy notes one important consequence of the transformation of football clubs from simple organisations for the arrangement of football matches into something more complex and culturally significant. By regularly attending a club's games, supporters "lend to it an identity which exceeds that constituted by those, namely the players, immediately implicated by the match". That identity is created, given its character, through the repeated participation and interaction of interested people over time around the matches. Accordingly, clubs come to have an existence and identity defined and constituted outside of the actual matches themselves, by the spectators rather than the players. Indeed, I would suggest that while this collective identity is informed by and responsive to the ever-changing collection of players that constitutes the actual team, it eventually comes to supersede it as the dominant factor in determining the particular nature of any given football club. One of my survey respondents put it as follows:

[A football club is] the collected actions and stories of the players and fans that have followed it through the years [...] A collection of stories, myths and legends based around a fairly silly competitive sport that bond generations of fans into partisan groups.

It is a familiar process and one not limited to football: repeated, interested interactions, through time, creating a thing of and for people that rolls on around the people themselves. Football historian David Goldblatt wrote along similar lines for the *Guardian* in 2020, echoing my question in the process.

What is a football club? The players and coaches come and go, owners and shareholders buy, sell up and move on, and they endure. Stadiums seem to embody them, until they are knocked down and relocated, but the club's existence is unbroken. Even the legal entity that constitutes a club can be expunged and liquidated, only for the same club to rise again in a new form. They can perform such alchemy because, in fact, football clubs are their supporters and the collective web of stories, memories and identities woven between themselves and the team over time: the stuff that makes football matter.

And as a point of comparison beyond football, consider John Berger's description of a French peasant village in the introduction to his novel *Pig Earth*. The village is:

The sum of all the social and personal relationships existing within it ... a living portrait of itself [constructed] not out of stone, but out of words, spoken and remembered: out of opinions, stories, eye-witness reports, legends, comments, and hearsay. ... [I]t is a continuous portrait; work on it never stops.

That agglomeration of intangible materials, that sense of constant, ongoing creation through participation, the idea of a living and continuous portrait — all this resonates. Perhaps, to football support's idealised child, the integration of the individual into this living portrait seems entirely natural. But picking up a new club as an adult, as I did when I started going to watch Dulwich Hamlet in 2010, exposes the workings a little. You become aware what this repeated, interested engagement does to a person. At first, you are there with perhaps one or two friends or family members; otherwise a stranger, surrounded by strangers. But over time this changes. You start to recognise people; you nod to them, then you chat with them. You buy a 50/50 ticket from the same person each time, and you make the same joke about never winning. "Next time!" You talk to people in the queue for the bar about the length of the queue for the bar; one of them sells you a fanzine. Later you write for that same fanzine, or perhaps you promise that you will but never get round to it. "Next time!" You laugh good-naturedly as the man who always stands by the bins tries to get his pet chant going again — and fails, again. "Next time!" You jump on a train for an away day and you see faces you recognise: some kind soul shuffles up to give you a seat, another hands you a bottle containing something mysterious and dark and sweet and — oof — strong. Later, you're all hugging each other as a goal goes in at the right end, or you're muttering darkly to one another as your useless defence and your useless goalkeeper get in each other's way again.

Obviously the particulars of this story will shift with context. At a Premier League game with allocated seating inside a tightly-managed, closely-stewarded stadium, a fan has much less control over the part of the matchday experience that actually involves the match. In, seat, bar, seat again, and out: it is with good reason that the sales pitch of the non-league evangelist usually begins "You can stand where you like, and you can have a pint while you watch." And of course for many people, for those fans not able to regularly attend their club's fixtures, their involvement with their club happens outside the games. Club identities are created, expressed, contested and enjoyed beyond the grounds: in pubs, on playgrounds, at work, within communities, and — constantly, endlessly, at times hellishly — online. A great humming tangle of human beings doing human things around, with, and through any given FC.

Kennedy develops the consequences of his observation along Marxist lines: the "ownership of football resembles a scale model of capitalism as Marx saw it". The very nature of football support — regular, repeated, interested physical attendance of fans — created a "readymade group of customers" and so, over time, the identity created by the fans (original emphasis):

> Becomes a product, a commodity made so by none other than the people who buy it. However, it is largely the case, not least in the United Kingdom, that the product is owned by a limited number of people with the financial wherewithal to purchase a stake in it. The football "experience" [...] is sold back to those who generate it in the first place; furthermore, the loyalty of fans allows for a monopolistic control over things such as ticket prices.

Of course, at the time most professional English clubs were emerging, the necessary capital (actual and social) to establish the club as a club — to buy land, to build a ground on that land — was to be found outside their largely working-class fanbases. Accordingly, as Kennedy notes, "the relationship between supporters and club owners is by its nature an antagonistic one between producers and those who have their hands on the means of production".

And it is not just Marxist analysis that brings out this antagonism. It's there in Bobby Robson's definition: here's what the club is, and here, just as importantly, is what it's not. That this is often understood as 'the fans' vs. 'the club' is a dispiriting though understandable act of surrender through shorthand. One of my survey respondents told me that "at the end of the day football is a business, and the chairman and players don't really care about the fans", while another said:

> *For me, it should be a representative of the local area, properly engaged with the local community, provider of facilities and general hub. [...] In the modern day, clubs at the highest levels have become more like brands or multi-*

national companies. TV money is all-important as clubs try to sell themselves in overseas territories to secure more sponsorship and merchandise sales. It is a sad state of affairs but indicative of the world in which we now live where trophies and profitability are the only barometers of success.

A brief history of one, two, or three football clubs

Wimbledon Football Club's community origin story began in 1889, when a park team made up of former pupils from the Old Central School formalised as Wimbledon Old Centrals. Initially, they played their games on Wimbledon Common, in south-west London, and they got changed in a local pub. For the majority of their early existence they were an amateur side, and from 1912 onwards they played their home games at Plough Lane, in the London borough of Merton.

Having spent several decades in the amateur Isthmian League, the club professionalised ahead of the 1964/65 season and joined the Southern League. Between 1974/75 and 1976/77, they won the league title three times in a row, after which they were elected into the Fourth Division of the Football League for the 1977/78 season. They yo-yoed between the Fourth and the Third Division for a few seasons, before achieving promotion to the Second Division in 1983/84, and then to the First in 1985/86. They finished sixth in their first top-flight season, and then in 1988 they won the FA Cup, beating heavy favourites Liverpool in the final. As football journalist David Conn puts it, Wimbledon's rise amounted to:

> One of English football's greatest and most important stories; the small club at the ragged ground playing its way from non-league, semi-professional football to scalping the game's biggest names. Proving that football is a shared passion, not a social hierarchy, that given the right spirit and circumstances all clubs belong with and have a chance against each other.

Few would argue with that, whatever their sympathies, but there were two important caveats to the story. The first, as Conn puts it: "if only you could think a little more fondly about the way they did it".

Wimbledon were nicknamed the 'Crazy Gang' and, if you were feeling charitable, then their style of football was ruggedly direct. If you weren't, and not many at the time were, then it was violently prehistoric. They took on and frequently overcame their opponents — almost all of them richer clubs with notionally stronger teams — by blending violence, both threatened and applied, with a direct style of play that horrified football's aesthetes. Lofted passes from back to front, a battle for the second ball, chances manufactured from the scraps: to its critics, the adoption of such an approach amounts to a de facto admission that a side neither knows nor cares how to play the game 'properly'. Wimbledon were unfashionable upstarts, urchins running their grubby fingers all over the silverware. If David Beasant saving John Aldridge's penalty in the '88 FA Cup final is the defining image of the Crazy Gang's achievements, then the defining image of their style is surely the famous picture of Vinnie Jones, his face a picture of malevolent concentration, reaching back and grabbing Paul Gascoigne by the genitals.[4]

I mention all this not to relitigate the arguments over style, but to illustrate that Wimbledon, even as their fairytale rise up the divisions was unfolding, were not universally adored or even respected by the wider footballing world. A *FourFourTwo* feature on "the 30 most hated teams in British football", written in 2017, is a useful illustration. MK Dons appeared in second place for all the obvious reasons that we'll get to later: "a tribute band claiming to be the original", a "synthetic club", a "club being broken down for parts".[5]

---

[4] In the interest of balance, we should note that condemnation was not universal. Here are the views of a local Labour councillor, Geoff Martin, excerpted in *When Saturday Comes* in 1989: "Sure, the club has got a direct style of play and they go in hard on the tackle, but what's wrong with that? I know for a fact that anyone who has played Sunday-morning park football will wonder what all the fuss is about." He held onto his seat in 1990.

[5] Don Revie's Leeds came in first, if you're wondering.

But Wimbledon '87/88 were just below them in fourth, their victory over the mighty Liverpool described as "football at its most agricultural". My stepdad, a Manchester United fan, tells the story of watching the '88 Cup final with friends, and all of them solemnly agreeing before kick-off that whatever their own allegiances, a Liverpool victory, though naturally loathsome on its own terms, was *necessary*. For the sake of football, the barbarians must be held at the gate. And so he had to watch, impassive and tight-lipped, as Kenny Dalglish's side were turned over by their notional inferiors, as Lawrie Sanchez and Beasant wrote themselves into legend, and it wasn't until he got home and rewatched the game on video that he could finally explode in laughter.

The other important point about Wimbledon's history in league football is that the club, even as they won promotion after promotion and made it all the way to Wembley, were in a state of constant financial precarity and so existential uncertainty. Over the years the club were linked with moves to Dublin, Manchester, Bristol, Wigan and Cardiff, as well as a merger with Crystal Palace. A move to Milton Keynes was first mooted in the 1970s as the new town was being established. The club's long-term chairman Sam Hammam moved the club out of Plough Lane in 1991, claiming it was too small, with a capacity of just under 16,000, and impossible to convert to an all-seater ground. This was and remains contested, but the club became tenants at Crystal Palace's Selhurst Park, six miles' walk away, and attendances suffered.

In 1997, Wimbledon FC were sold to two Norwegian investors, Kjell Inge Røkke and Bjørn Rune Gjelsten. Røkke, who had made his money in the fishing business, had previous experience in football club ownership, having invested in Norwegian club Molde FK in the early '90s; his business partner Gjelsten was a former powerboat racing champion. It is widely believed that they bought the club on the understanding that a move to Dublin was all but certain to go ahead, along with the opportunity to build a new stadium-casino development. This turned out not to be the case, and after the move was vetoed by the Irish Football Association they were left owning a club without a home. Hammam had sold the Plough Lane site to Safeway in 1998, and while a supermarket never actually got built, the stadium had been demolished. The team's results declined throughout the late '90s and at the end of the 1999/2000 season they were relegated back down to the second tier.

Enter 'Stadium MK'. The public face of the consortium, a record producer named Pete Winkelman, burst into the footballing consciousness with a messianic glint in his eye: he came to share the good news of Milton Keynes, which was by his account the biggest city in Europe without professional football.[6] This wasn't just about bringing the people's game to the people, however: the consortium was backed by Wal-Mart-owned supermarket chain Asda and furniture giant Ikea. A proposed retail complex on greenfield land could only get planning permission if part of the development amounted to a civic good. Flatpack furniture wasn't enough; a flatpack football club would do nicely. The consortium approached Luton Town, Crystal Palace, Barnet, and at one stage suggested merging Wimbledon and Queens Park Rangers and moving them both out of London, before eventually reaching an agreement in 2001 with Wimbledon's new chairman Charles Koppel.

Wimbledon's board approved the move in July 2001, but the Football League rejected the idea: according to the League's chief executive, David Burns, "To allow the move would have created a precedent at odds with the history of football in this country." Koppel took legal advice and appealed, and the matter went first to arbitration, then back to the Football League, and finally to a three-person independent panel convened by the FA. This panel comprised Raj Parker, a commercial solicitor; Steve Stride, operations director of Premier League club Aston Villa; and Alan Turvey, the chairman of the semi-professional Isthmian League. Against the league's

---

[6] As a point of pedantic order, Milton Keynes is not in fact a city: applications to the Civic Honours competitions in 2000, 2002, and 2012 all failed. The practical consequences of this for Milton Keynes' residents are minimal; the City Centre is still universally known as the City Centre.

original decision, and the wishes of the protesting fans, on 28 May 2002 they voted 2-1 to allow the move (the dissenting vote is understood to have come from Turvey). Their published reasoning pays particular heed to the monetary losses being made by the club, the claims by the owners that they had no alternative but to move away, and the enthusiastic sales pitch from the interested parties in Milton Keynes. The board and shareholders were to be given the "opportunity to put the club on a more solid financial footing". As for the fans, they could take advantage of Milton Keynes' excellent transport links. Perhaps special buses could be laid on.

Having protested vehemently throughout the process, Wimbledon's fans convened to discuss the future. On 30 May 2002 Kris Stewart, chair of the Wimbledon Independent Supporters Association, stood up in front of a meeting of more than 1,000 supporters and told them "I'm tired of fighting, I just want to watch football." The early steps of forming AFC Wimbledon had already been taken — impishly, the official paperwork filed with the FA includes a foundation date of 1889 — and by the middle of June, the new club was under the control of the supporters' trust, had arranged to share a ground with non-league Kingstonian, had secured a place in the Combined Counties League (the ninth tier of English football), and was holding open trials for players on Wimbledon Common. Nearly 5,000 fans turned up to their first fixture, on 10 July, a 4-0 away loss to Sutton United.

Wimbledon FC played one more season at Selhurst Park in front of home crowds as low as 700. The club were declared insolvent and entered administration in June 2003, and were bought out by Winkelman, eventually making the move to Milton Keynes in September of the same year. They were relegated to League One, the third tier, at the end of the 2003/04 season, and over the summer they emerged from administration with a new badge, new colours, and a new name: they were now the Milton Keynes Dons.

As Wimbledon had years before, AFC Wimbledon embarked on a sharp rise through the non-league pyramid. They were promoted five times in their first nine seasons, securing a return to league football and the fourth tier in 2011. Both teams are currently in League One, the third tier: at the end of the 2020/21 season, AFC avoided relegation and finished in 19th, while MK Dons finished in a safe, unspectacular 13th. But the season brought one moment of triumph for AFC: in November 2020, they played their first game at their new stadium, the second Plough Lane, just a few minutes walk from the site of their previous ground.

Earlier I suggested that the part of a club's identity constituted by the fans as *fans* might be considered the most important part. Perhaps the response to the split of so many football fans beyond Wimbledon, fans with little to no time for these violent, agricultural upstarts, serves to illustrate this point. As noted in the introduction, nearly two-thirds of my survey respondents identified AFC Wimbledon as the continuation of Wimbledon, suggesting that the power of making and maintaining the club lay with, and continues to lie with, the supporters. Fewer than 15% identified MK Dons as the continuation.

MK Dons are technically the continuation but of course, by moving location and changing names they're anything but. AFCW isn't a traditional phoenix club in this respect, as it formed differently to most and in the wake of MKD, but I believe it's closest to the truth to say they're a continuation of WFC.

Despite the official continuation status of MK, the fan ownership and local status of AFC Wimbledon makes them the closer definition.

At times, football can seem powered by grudges, and so it is, I think, significant that Wimbledon's general reputation does not appear to have prevented fans of other clubs responding negatively to the move. What was unusual about Wimbledon, then, is not that 'the club' and 'the fans' were in opposition: that is a widely understood and widely shared problem. It's the end of this process; indeed, it's the fact that it ended. Instead of a takeover, or a rapprochement, or everybody just rubbing along as best they could in conditions of mutual but not-quite-destructive antagonism, the club split into two. An unprecedented severance, but along familiar and relatable fault lines.

Chapter Two:
From WFC to AFC and MKD

A unique solution to a unique problem

In chapter one, I suggested that it is the regular, repeated attendance of fans that serves to make and maintain a crucial part of the identity of a football club. But this is not the only way of conceptualising a football club, and during the 2001/02 season Wimbledon's owners attempted to advance an alternative theory. While the relationship between the club hierarchy and the vast majority of Wimbledon's fans had almost completely broken down by the time of the move, there was a point early in the process where the ownership attempted to reach out beyond what they hoped was a noisy minority and connect with some quieter but more persuadable fans. To this end, the club produced a glossy, 32-page, full-colour booklet called *A Unique Solution to a Unique Problem*, subtitled *Why Wimbledon Football Club has to move to Milton Keynes*. That 'has to' is key here: this is not a question of desirability, but of existential necessity. Indeed, it's not a question at all.

It is, with hindsight, a fascinating document, and one to which history has not been kind. It is worth considering in some detail here as it is not just an intervention in the argument but a manifesto of sorts, a statement about what a football club is and is not. "I realise that many of our fans currently consider the idea of a move to Milton Keynes to be inappropriate," wrote Koppel in the introduction, rather underselling things. "I hope that fans will read it."

The booklet opens with a double-page spread showing an artist's impression of Wimbledon's promised new stadium, a gleaming bowl in black and gold, surrounded by concentric circles of parked cars hooping outwards to a ring of ominous black monoliths.[7] The overall effect is to suggest that Wimbledon would be taking up residence in the 23rd century — Milton Keynes: city of the future — or perhaps inside an expensive designer watch. This vaguely science-fictional air is reinforced by a quote from an anonymous 'Wimbledon fan, SW16':

> I know what we are trying to do and if moving to Milton Keynes or Mars means keeping the club alive then good luck to you.

The first few pages of the booklet are devoted to setting out the state of play as the club saw it: revenue lost thanks to the Selhurst Park tenancy; the perilous financial situation; the inability to build a fanbase around Selhurst Park; the asserted lack of a "substantial supporter base" in Merton. Then comes the case for Milton Keynes, which is made in three distinct phases.

The first, and largest, is devoted to demolishing the idea that Wimbledon could move back to Plough Lane. Quotes from a study by FPD Savills, a real estate services provider, are overlaid on pictures of the abandoned Plough Lane site: a pile of rubbish; the hollowed out and windowless executive lounge; a horse grazing in front of overgrown terraces. But it's not just Plough Lane that will not, cannot work. There is nowhere else in Merton. Or anywhere else in London. Or even anywhere near London: one map shows boroughs as far away as Crawley in West Sussex, Waverley in Surrey, Maidenhead in Berkshire, and Dartford in Kent, all with "no suitable sites for development of a football stadium". One site is dismissed as "being driven by commercial developers", a project "based primarily on developers extracting land value NOT linked to the benefits of football". Imagine such a thing.

---

[7]   Having spent quite some time looking at this picture, I think they're supposed to be multi-storey car parks. This makes sense, as cars are very important in Milton Keynes. Walking around roundabouts takes ages.

The thrust of this argument, along with a fair amount of the detail, was disputed by Wimbledon fans at the time. We don't need to recap the arguments here: the opening of AFC Wimbledon's new ground in November 2020, just a short walk from the original site of Plough Lane, does the job rather neatly.

With great semiotic subtlety, the booklet moves on to a picture of some gleaming green fields: "Milton Keynes – A Real Opportunity". A 28,000-seater stadium! Conference and exhibition facilities! A 200-bed hotel! Car parking for 2,000! And a "football frenzy waiting to happen", with "full backing from the city's political, business and sporting interests". It is striking that the authors of the booklet were unable to find any fans from Milton Keynes, potential early adopters, to bear explicit witness to this frenzy, instead relying on the word of local politicians. The best the booklet can manage is a picture of grinning children holding up pieces of card: "IT'S" "A" "FOOT" "BALL" "THING" "MK THIS WAY!" At least they were holding the cards in the right order.

The case for Milton Keynes ends on another gesture towards the impossibility of doing things any other way, one that presumably came as a surprise to Wimbledon's fans:

> ... some believe that if Milton Keynes needs and deserves a professional team of its own, one of the currently minor teams in the new city should rise through the leagues and become a major force. But this lacks any reality. History dictates that this is not how other teams develop ...

Imagine such a thing.

Time has falsified most of the specific claims, and rendered the rest moot. The most interesting section of the booklet comes after the practicalities, when Wimbledon's hierarchy attempt to make their case that Wimbledon in Milton Keynes will be the "same club" as Wimbledon in Wimbledon. In doing so, they address a fundamental problem, for with a few exceptions beloved by those who set pub quizzes, English football clubs are named for the places in which they are located. Anybody considering moving a club, then, is immediately faced with a problem: do they stick with the old name, and look peculiar, or change that as well, and gravely weaken their claim to be the same club.

Initially, Wimbledon's owners were insistent that they would remain the owners of a club called Wimbledon. "The club's move to Milton Keynes would NOT mean the establishment of a new club". And how would everybody be able to tell? Well:

> If and when the Club moves to Milton Keynes the Club will:
> - Still be called Wimbledon FC
> - Continue to play in its famous yellow and blue colours;
> - Continue to have the same never say die attitude!

Despite the optimistic exclamation mark, none of these claims proved to be true.[8] But we can see the thread of the argument: just because the club will be somewhere else, doesn't mean it will be some*thing* else. Or, to put it another way, the component parts of a club that matter, that give that club its identity, are the external tangibles of shirt, name, badge, and so on, along with various behaviours: that "never say die" attitude. If it looks like Wimbledon, and if it walks and talks and plays like Wimbledon, why, it must be Wimbledon, whatever the map says. It amounts to a claim about the nature of a football club: its location is neither necessary nor sufficient.

Club names, shirt colours, crests: these things are important to football fans. Cardiff City fans protested vigorously when their majority shareholder Vincent Tan changed the club's kit from blue to red, simultaneously reconfiguring the badge to incorporate a red Welsh dragon. The club announced at the time that:

---

[8]   On a symbolic level, perhaps the most pointed rejection of the owners' case came from Elizabeth Beresford, resident of Merton and creator of the Wombles, the children's TV show from which Wimbledon took their nickname and from which I have taken the title of this book. Wimbledon's mascot Wandle the Womble, first introduced in 2000 and named for a tributary of the Thames in south London, was seen no more after the license expired in 2003. In 2006, after a naming competition judged by Beresford herself, Haydon the Womble made his debut on the AFC Wimbledon touchline: Haydons Road is the train station closest to Plough Lane, old and new.

> The changes to the home kit and badge introduced as a consequence of the investment package are designed to help the club to develop its brand and to allow it to expand its appeal to as wide an audience as possible, with a view to delivering local success via an international and diverse market.

The change was implemented in 2012, as a part of Tan's wider investment into the club; the new owner claimed that red was a luckier colour than blue. By 2014, surveys of supporters showed 85% were in favour of changing the kit back. Protest marches were numbering the thousands, and plans for a boycott of season tickets were under way. In December 2014, Tan announced that "Protesting will not make me change my mind," and called on the fans to "think carefully and support the club so that we can get promoted to the Premier League." But come the New Year, apparently on the advice of his mother, he reversed his decision. Cardiff City went back to blue in January 2015 and have stayed in blue ever since.

Not all kit changes result in protests: there is a rather endearing thread through English football's history of teams changing their colours, generally at the behest of their manager, in order to more closely resemble one of the great European sides. In 1971, in a nod to AC Milan, John Bond introduced black stripes onto Bournemouth's previously solid red shirts; 10 years earlier, Don Revie clad Leeds United in white in honour of the Real Madrid team that dominated the European Cup in the 1950s.[9] More straightforwardly, according to legend Bill Shankly dressed Liverpool all in red to make them look as terrifying as possible: "The players looked like giants. And we played like giants."

Name changes are rarer, and the most notable recent example came in 2013, when Hull City dropped 'Association Football Club' from their name and registered as 'Hull City Tigers Ltd'. The club's owners, Assem Allam, told the *Guardian* that he planned to go further and drop "City" as well, claiming that the word was

---

[9] It has been suggested that Real Madrid chose white for their shirts and shorts after club officials watched a cricket match while touring England, which lends this whole chromatic dance a pleasing circularity.

redundant and too heavily associated with other clubs. Hull would become 'Hull Tigers', as "the shorter the name the more powerful — think of Coca-Cola, Twitter, Apple". He also claimed that if he were in charge of Manchester City he would "change the name to Manchester Hunter." Fans protested, and the protests sharpened when Allam, in response to the formation of a fan group called 'City Till I Die', told the *Independent* "They can die as soon as they want, as long as they leave the club for the majority who just want to watch good football." Eventually his application for a formal name change was rejected by the FA, and the plan appears to have been abandoned.

Changes to crests are generally met with less overt opprobrium, though the removal of 'Football Club' from Manchester United's badge in 1998 is still a source of discontent for some United fans. Everton fans complained in numbers when the Latin motto *Nil Satis Nisi Optimum* — nothing but the best is good enough — was removed from their crest in 2013, and it was restored after a season's absence. More recently, in 2018 Leeds United's owners proposed replacing the white rose with a headless man doing the 'Leeds salute': thumping a clenched fist into his chest. Online objections, which ran into the tens of thousands, focused partly on the perceived disrespect for history and tradition, but also, and very strongly, on the peculiar look of the thing. Some felt it looked troublingly totalitarian, others that it belonged in a computer game that couldn't afford to license official logos, and a few noted that 'it looks like a Gaviscon ad'. The redesign was eventually ditched.

Had Wimbledon's owners decided to solve their business conundrum with an aggressive rebrand — purple and yellow hoops, Vinnie Jones' face on the badge, a name change to the Transpontine Wombles — we can assume that Wimbledon's fans would have mobilised in similar fashion to the protestors in Cardiff and Hull. It is not clear whether the idea of a new club would have taken hold in the same fashion, however. That will doubtless come down, in large part, to the fact that it is easier to imagine a new club in a place that is being vacated: Vincent Tan, as far as I can tell, never considered taking his club off to pastures new. Let the protest fit the crime: you complain about a new kit by wearing an old one; you complain about a lost club by starting a new one.[10]

For the club's owners, the dire financial position explained the practical need for the move, but the contention that the club would remain the same provided a justification for the otherwise unthinkable. By this understanding, the club consisted in these traditional, transplantable, cosmetic components — shirt, crest, name — and in the intangibles that had surrounded the club, the relocated craziness of the Crazy Gang. The club would still be the club; therefore, the club should move to protect the club. For the protesting fans, meanwhile, the whole question of the club's identity was almost entirely contingent on place: name, badge and suchlike all followed as a matter of course and historical observance, while sporting, financial and administrative inconveniences could all be borne. As one of my interviewees, Charlie, put it:

> There was a famous statement by Koppel, who said "So-called fans would rather see us playing back at Plough Lane in the Fourth Division than playing in Milton Keynes in the Premier League. Those people aren't true fans." And you say: you couldn't have that more wrong if you tried. 'Cos you know, as any football fan will tell you, the exact opposite is clearly the case. If you would rather support your football team, and its sense of belonging, and its place, and community and all the rest of it, at whatever level, then yeah, you are a true fan. If you need to be in the Premier League to give a toss, you're not.

Indeed, looking at the Wimbledon story, we might conclude that location is the only thing about a football club that cannot possibly be allowed to change. It is the ultimate *is*, the ultimate *should*. If a football team is given its identity by the repeated and interested attendance of its fans, over time, then it is secured in that identity

---

10   FC United of Manchester stand as an interesting dissent here, and I will consider them more in chapter five.

if and only if those fans can continue to attend the same place. That is, I think, not just a question of practicality and access, although it's not clear if the special buses were ever laid on.

Football grounds are not just the stage for the experience, but an intimate part of the experience; they are not just places to watch but places that shape the experience of watching. Many football fans develop a topophilic relationship with their club's ground that cannot be explained by the aesthetic appeal or utility of that ground: as was said of Wimbledon's original Plough Lane, 'a dump, but *our* dump'. Such attachment suggests something stronger, more productive, more enriching than mere attendance. Something like home-making. While I was poking this chapter into shape, I came across an essay by josie sparrow on William Morris' Red House, which clarifies beautifully this sense of creative mutuality between people and place.

> We dwell in our doing, and our doing makes the places that we dwell. Our inhabiting creates what is habitual; likewise, our habits unfold within and around the places we inhabit. Everything is situated, everything is relational, everything is in process — and so there can be no absolute beginnings, only points of departure. These points are accretions of moments, of memories; they are places that shelter and nourish. They are sites of folding-in that make unfolding possible.

And then: "We might call them homes."

Practically speaking, the Wimbledon split centred on the immediate interests of the two parties: the desire to run a profitable business set against the desire to watch a local football team. But it became a contest between two competing ideas of what a football club should be, how it should behave, what should and should not be the case. It is perhaps up for debate how far the owners were actually committed to this idea of what a football club should be, and whether they were in fact much more exercised by the need to say whatever might rescue their rapidly curdling investment. But even if this is the case, it is still telling that they felt they had to have this argument: that they had to meet their opponents and make their case on this terrain. Even for those who would treat a football club as only a business, lip service must be paid to the idea that it is something more.

The decision

The final decision on Wimbledon's fate came on 28 May 2002, though some fans had been tipped the nod the day before and were able to attend FA headquarters to protest. On the day, the commission published a summary of their decision. They needed 67 pages to move a football club from one place to a distant other, but paragraph 128 immediately leapt from the page and into footballing infamy.

> Furthermore, resurrecting the Club from its ashes as, say, 'Wimbledon Town' is, with respect to those supporters who would rather that happened so that they could go back to the position the Club started in 113 years ago, not in the wider interests of football.

Although the idea of a new club had already been discussed and was in the early stages of planning, Ivor Heller, who would go on to become AFC Wimbledon's commercial director, later referred to this particular statement as "the greatest catalyst we could have wished for".[11]

Interestingly, the only specific negative consequence that the commission identified for football's wider interests — that is, beyond the consequences for Wimbledon's owners and fans — is that another club, "most probably Brentford FC", would have to be promoted to take Wimbledon's place, and that this promotion would come "not on its own sporting merit but as a result of WFC's predicament". The committee asserted that "the pyramid structure

---

[11] In one respect, the commission was correct: Wimbledon Town would not have been a great name. AFC Wimbledon is much better. Though honestly, I'm not entirely sure why. Initially I wrote, quite confidently, that the power of the name 'AFC' comes from the fact that every time you say it, you're really saying 'A Football Club'. But I have since lost faith in this theory, which is why it's down here in a footnote.

is better served by giving WFC the opportunity to survive, albeit in a new conurbation ... rather than condemning it to liquidation and extinction in Merton".

Beyond Wimbledon fans, and beyond the obvious grubbiness of the whole process, it was the sanctity of the pyramid structure that was the main concern of many non-Wimbledon fans. And it is easy to see why: abstractly, and leaving to one side a whole range of complicating factors, every football pyramid is a beautiful thing, and England's runs wider and deeper than any other in the world. The very best team in the country threaded down to every one of the lowliest, with only sporting questions keeping them apart — lots and lots of sporting questions, but the principle is there. And at the end of every season a rebalancing, a great and terrible shiver, as clubs are judged and sorted. Some go climbing up season on season in search of somebody to give them a game, while others sink and sink again, taking memories of lost greatness to clubs that have never known greatness of their own; the fallen thrown down among the yet to rise. And each of these clubs is rooted in and a creation of their community, and so each village, every suburb, all the towns and cities are stitched together, tied to one another, a vast slow-shifting ecology of hope and pride, Uniteds and Albions, despair and boredom, Wanderers and Citys, floodlights and drizzle and large sensible coats. The vitality is key: the hope and joy of movement up and the fear and despair of movement down.

At the end of any season, each club's — each community's — position in the pyramid is the story of that season, but it is also the story of all their seasons up to that point, one after the other, up and down and down and up, the entire history of the club leading them to that precise position. The place that they and only they have earned. Sporting merit, structurally enforced: you get what you deserve. And Milton Keynes, so the suggestion went, just hadn't put the work in.[12]

12   Once, slightly drunk, I spent an hour insisting to a very patient, very polite man that the English footballing pyramid would, in a fair world, be considered a monument of cultural majesty on a par with Machu Picchu. We'd only just met, and I suggested we petition UNESCO together. I never

The actual functioning of the English pyramid is significantly less panglossian, and vast monetary imbalances keep the pyramid stratified, every club picking on the ones below. There are licensing and stadium criteria for clubs that must be satisfied in order to achieve promotion, not to mention associated increases in wages and the need for further training. Plus, of course, the orderly up and down movement of football clubs as football clubs is disrupted whenever a mishandled club enters administration: points deductions for financial irregularities send some teams down and keep others up in spite of their onfield performances.

This is what the committee professed to be hoping to avoid, yet in hindsight, it sounds like a pretty feeble attempt at a gotcha. *Ah ha! You claim you love the pyramid and sporting merit so much, but wouldn't this also violate the principles of sporting merit? Checkmate, Wombles.* Football clubs don't often wink out of existence entirely, but it has happened, and the pyramid adjusts with an extra promotion spot here or one fewer relegation spot there. And the more likely scenario — administration, a relegation or two, and an eventual buyout at a much lower price — is sadly familiar, almost commonplace. At the start of the 2019/20 season, Bury FC were expelled from the Football League after collapsing financially; at the end of it, Wigan Athletic were docked 12 points for entering administration. In the former case, League One was contested with 23 teams and one fewer relegation spot than normal; in the latter, Luton Town were the beneficiaries of Wigan's drop into the relegation zone.[13] But in this case, the idea that Brentford might

---

saw him again. And it only occurred to me a few hours later that a better comparison might have been the actual Pyramids.

[13] Following the collapse of Bury FC, a group of fans have formed Bury AFC, and this phoenix club has been accepted into the North West Counties Football League in the ninth tier of the pyramid. However, Bury FC, at the time of writing not a member of any league, are still issuing statements: one such, in August 2020, announced "there is ONLY ONE BURY FOOTBALL CLUB" (original capitals), condemned local journalists and Greater Manchester Police, and then proceeded to castigate the BBC over reported plans to remove Rule Britannia from the

pinch a promotion place they hadn't quite earned was deemed to be more disruptive than a Championship club disappearing in one place and reappearing in another. The place was not seen as relevant.

But on its own, this would not do. One of the more intriguing themes of the commission's report is that the case for moving to Milton Keynes is made in terms not just practical but explicitly moral. We learn (all emphasis mine) that "Milton Keynes provides a suitable and *deserving* opportunity"; that Peter Winkelman believed Milton Keynes "*merited* having a football club". Later, as we come to the decision, we hear that Milton Keynes has been "*starved* of First Division football", and that the case for moving is "unquestionably *deserving*". That "unquestionably" sits rather awkwardly with the fact that the committee itself could only come to a majority decision, but summary reports are written by the victors.

This moral throughline is interesting not just because it tells us that Winkelman absolutely nailed his pitch.[14] It implies that the practical benefits identified by the committee did not add up to a sufficiently persuasive case in themselves; that the committee didn't feel able to say: *Look, this will save the business, and the balance of expert opinion is that going back to Plough Lane is completely impossible, and that's your lot.* Or, perhaps more likely, that it might not be a good idea to be seen to say just that. That, after all, might have served as effective permission "for franchise football to arrive on these shores", an outcome the commission repeatedly states they are desperate to avoid. They needed to construct a positive, non-business case *for* the move; only then could the extraordinary decision be justified.

Last Night of the Proms. "What's left to sanction, Hymns or the Bible", asked the club, concluding with a more-or-less quote from Voltaire: "IT IS SAID THAT TO BE A GOOD PATRIOT ONE MUST OFTEN BE THE ENEMY OF OTHER PEOPLES". Capital letters Bury's, not Voltaire's.

[14] To quote the summary again: "His energy and commitment to the project were self-evident" and his enthusiasm "for Milton Keynes itself, was almost infectious, and obviously genuine." Sceptical readers might raise an eyebrow at "almost".

What could it mean, then, for a town to deserve a football club? That a potential fanbase existed in Milton Keynes seems fairly inarguable, even if a little exaggeration can be detected in the club's case. Winkelman claimed and the commission accepted that Milton Keynes was the biggest urban concentration in Europe without a professional football team to call its own, and the committee noted in their decision that the "potential fan base is huge. Eight million people live within one hour's drive, and 2.2 million within half an hour's drive." They neglect to mention, however, that this hour's drive includes a number of locations already well-provisioned with professional football clubs: Coventry, Northampton, Cambridge, Oxford, Luton, Watford, Wycombe, Barnet ... indeed, an hour's drive south and kind traffic would have put you within walking distance of White Hart Lane or Highbury. Arguing for the move, Wimbledon's owners asserted that: "Most fans spend over an hour getting to see matches in big cities". They don't clarify why any fan already travelling that hour from Milton Keynes to any other club would simply throw their preferred team over the moment a new one arrived.[15]

But even if we allow for potential interest, and for an unusually un-footballed catchment area, there is more to deserving something than simply lacking it, wanting it and being able to make use of it. There is a normative heft to the idea, a sense that things ought to be this way. That a wrong is here to be righted. And to make this case the commission held up the possibility of a new Wimbledon elsewhere against Wimbledon as it existed at that moment. Then they found south London wanting.

Hindsight again rather renders this ridiculous, but one of the key criteria advanced by the committee is the idea that "WFC's links or roots in its community are of a nature that can be [...] retained by WFC and MKSC [Milton Keynes Stadium Consortium], albeit in a new location". The committee states that they "do not believe, with all due respect, that the Club's links with the community around

---

[15]   More on what the people of Milton Keynes thought of all this in chapter four.

the Plough Lane site or in Merton are so profound, or the roots go so deep, that they will not survive a necessary transplant to ensure WFC's survival." The horticultural metaphor there is suggestive: the roots are shallow, the soil is thin, and there isn't much sunlight; the club must be repotted or it will die.

The evidence advanced for this shallowness of roots appears to be based largely on the submissions of the club's owners, who presumably had access to the relevant data:

> What is unusual about WFC fans is that they do not seem to come from a single geographical area. Indeed, the vast majority of WFC fans do not live in Merton or Wimbledon. Twenty percent of current season ticket holders live in Merton and 10% in Wimbledon. [WFC's] relatively low Merton residents supporters base and its time at Selhurst Park do not suggest that it is the "heart and soul" of its community.

I do not propose here to rehash the arguments over these points, though one factor that might complicate this picture seems immediately obvious: that those fans content to maintain season tickets at Selhurst Park might be those more happy to travel in general. Heading to Selhurst Park rather than Plough Lane is perhaps not much of an adjustment for a fan already travelling in from outside London, but it's a profound upheaval for anybody that used to walk to the game. In any case, nobody was arguing that this was a happy football club. But this was a snapshot of a fanbase taken after 11 years of tenancy at Selhurst Park, not to mention much agitation against the moves to Dublin and Milton Keynes. Indeed, you could argue that Wimbledon hadn't really existed happily or as it should have existed for all of those 11 years, and so assessing the interest in Merton on the basis of the figures from that moment could never have been reflective of the potential interest.

The moral calculus is made explicit in one of the appended schedules to the summary decision, a letter from an anonymous fan to Charles Koppel entitled 'A Supporter for Milton Keynes'. This fan describes themselves as having been converted from an anti-Milton Keynes position by the arguments of the board, and states:

> The people of Wimbledon do not deserve a football club and the apathy they show to the Club is unbelievable. I drive two hours to get to every home game and have been doing so for as long as I can remember. [...] If Wimbledon wants to reach the Premiership again and to stay there then this can only be achieved with a move to Milton Keynes. [...] I would hate to lose the name because of the history and tradition associated with it but I do wonder if Wimbledon Town deserves to have a football club.

The commission doesn't quite go so far, but it does extrapolate from the alleged lack of interest in that particular moment that there is no prospect of improvement. The burden here is placed almost entirely on the fans: they are expected to travel out of their way to a ground that isn't theirs, to watch a poor team play poor football, and to hand over money to evidently uninterested owners who are actively trying to move their team away ... and when they balk at any or all of that, it is taken as evidence that they don't really deserve a football team! The underlying presumption is that football fans should offer nothing beyond unthinking, unengaged, almost reflexive devotion, and that the absence of such demonstrates the absence of support both actual and potential, present and future. We should note that while Wimbledon's attendances were always small by the standards of both the old Division One and then the Premier League, they were hardly insignificant: their last season in the Premier League had an attendance high of more than 26,000 and an average of about 17,000.

Beyond this claim about fans' dedication, there is another general principle being advanced: an idea of what football clubs should look like and what they should be trying to do. On the one hand, Wimbledon-as-they-were: homeless, in debt, undersupported, unapologetically unglamorous, and burdened with fans that, as far as the commission was concerned, either didn't really care or were content to shuffle back to the anonymity of the lower leagues.

On the other, the Wimbledon-that-could-be: the heart of a grateful community; partnered with Asda and Ikea; playing inside a shiny new stadium; and always twirling, twirling, twirling towards the Premier League. Is a football club really a football club if it isn't always trying to be the biggest and the best?

And so the commission had found the formula that would allow them to ignore the wishes of the majority of the club's fans, the previous decision of the Football League, and the long-standing principles of the game's overarching structure: a place that apparently doesn't want its club; another place that notionally deserves it; and a financial and logistical pickle sufficiently alarming that a move from the former to the latter can be presented as the only workable option. The practical case always made a certain amount of business sense, of course; nobody was pretending that Wimbledon weren't in serious financial trouble or that there was a painless and cheap path back to Merton. But it's the moral argument that allows the committee to not only reach its conclusion, but to then, audaciously, plead for its necessity: "To refuse permission we believe would be stretching the overarching principles too far, and would be more than is reasonably necessary … These principles which are a fundamental feature of the English game will not be violated by permission being granted in this case, which we regard as unique and unquestionably deserving."

In light of these fundamental features of the English game, let us return again to the idea of 'the wider interests of football'. For (two-thirds of) the commission, these were served by Wimbledon FC taking what the owners claimed to be its most likely path towards financial solvency in the short term, and then sporting competitiveness in the medium to long term, here understood as trying to reach the Premier League. No fan would ever really complain about either state of affairs — though it is noticeable that fans of teams regularly promoted to and relegated from the Premier League often find the seasons competing at the top of the Championship far more enjoyable than those spent struggling at the bottom of the Premier League — but it is clear that the important alignment here is between the interests of football and the interests of football club owners.

The commission dismissed the counterpoint: that the club should stay in the place of its origins, even if it had to undergo financial and competitive collapse. Kris Stewart, chair of the Wimbledon Independent Supporters Association (WISA), was asked by the commission if he could choose between life in Milton Keynes and death in Wimbledon, and replied that "he regarded both as death". Stewart's now-famous lament that preceded the foundation of AFC Wimbledon — "I just want to watch football" — comes with the implicit but fundamental conditions: in Wimbledon, with Wimbledon, as Wimbledon. This point of view considers the wider interests of football to be served by each club having its place within the community that founded it, connected to and available to the people that have nurtured and created it, whether that club is in the Premier League, the Isthmian Premier League, or bouncing around somewhere between the two. A further implication: it is better for a club to fail as both a financial and as a sporting entity, then be rebuilt in the knowledge that things may never be quite as good again, than it is for the club to leave its community.

An actual conflict of the scale, intensity and existential import of that which consumed Wimbledon is not an inevitable consequence of this tension and, in most cases, the practical interests of the fans and the owners tend to point in the same direction (even if, as previously noted, a majority of fans remain leery as to their club's owner's motivations). But nevertheless, we can see here two distinct and at least potentially incompatible answers to the question of what a football club is, and what it is for. And the ultimate implication of the fans' position is that a football club isn't really for trying to win football games at all; at least, not if those games aren't being watched by the fans. Victories may be the moment-to-moment preoccupation of the team and the game-by-game desire of the supporters — football would make no sense otherwise — but there are important preconditions.

Chapter Three:
Breaking and making a football club

It is impossible to speak precisely of the split at Wimbledon without drowning oneself in caveats.[16] Neither side was monolithic at the time and positions shifted through the crisis — indeed, speaking of them as distinct 'sides' perhaps implies a cleanliness that is unjustified. And since the split, both new clubs have gone on evolving. It is evident that a significant number of Wimbledon fans switched allegiance to AFC, but there were also Wimbledon fans that became MK Dons fans, Wimbledon fans who gave up on supporting anybody, fans of other teams or no team in particular that latched onto both AFC Wimbledon and MK Dons, and now, years later, both AFC and MK Dons have acquired new fans through the ordinary business of being a football club. Football and life are both messy and unpredictable things, and the Hornbyite ideal of the football fan — forever committed, forever obsessed, forever monogamous — is undercut by the many complications of the real world. This chapter will, therefore, rely on a certain amount of generalisation, for which I beg preemptive forgiveness.

---

[16] Honestly, I'm not even sure that 'split' is the best word: it doesn't quite seem to capture the emotive, human nature of what happened. Disentanglement might be better, or perhaps even divorce: one side citing adultery, the other desertion. Other words that have been put to me as I've been writing this book: movement, departure, betrayal, abandonment, 'the great fucking-off' ... I went with 'bifurcation' in the title of my dissertations, which looking back seems a little unnecessary. Here I'll stick with 'split' because I can't think of anything easily and obviously better.

In any case, the idea that this was an argument between two clearly delineated and static 'sides' is not a sustainable one. The rigid, almost manichaean division of a football club into 'us' and 'them' is a useful gloss and at times entirely appropriate, but often fails to capture the messy reality of football clubs as social and cultural institutions, and fans as active agents both within and upon those institutions.[17] She wasn't talking about football, but anthropologist Susan Wright put it nicely:

> Cultural identities are not inherent, bounded or static; they are dynamic, fluid and constructed situationally, in particular places and times [...] 'cultures' are not, nor ever were, naturally bounded entities.

One manifestation of this dynamism is the way opposition to the move among Wimbledon's fan base spread and intensified over time. Though long-rumoured, the move was formally announced in a letter to all season ticket holders in August 2001, and was presented as, essentially, a done deal. It is unclear whether the club's owners expected the fans simply to shrug and accept the decision, but the response was immediate and negative: as Wimbledon ran out to play Birmingham City on the first day of the 2001/02 season, a number of the home fans released black balloons from the stands.

But while the response from the fans was nearly universally negative, it was not entirely unified, both around the question of how serious this was and how best to respond to it. One of my interviewees, Charlie, who attended his first game at Selhurst Park aged eight, recalls that there was a range of strengths of feeling in those early weeks:

> Between the extremist 'we will do anything we can to prevent this happening by any means necessary' through to 'I will write some strongly-worded letters'. A lot of people at those

---

[17]   And of course, we should note that not everybody watching a game while wearing a suit is malignant, careless or uninterested, and that many boardrooms contain people that are honest and enthusiastic and want nothing but the best for their respective club. Even if they don't always know quite how to get it.

first few games would actually say sit down, shut up and support the team. It'll never happen.

Charlie was involved in organising the protests through the season. He says that they initially didn't consider turning their backs at a game, because:

> If it's just a fairly small percentage it's a big PR own goal, because the club can go 'Well, look, it's only 20% of you idiots complaining' [...] If you think back to the previous September, and we'd said that was the protest, I think a lot of people wouldn't have turned their backs.

But throughout the season, as it became clear that this was a serious plan and as the club, per Charlie, "paint[ed] themselves as bigger and bigger villains", support for the protests spread. At one of the last home games of the season, the call finally went out for the crowd to turn their backs on play:

> And I remember looking over my shoulder at that point, and it was quite a spine tingling moment [...] 90%, at least 90%. And I remember thinking 'we've won'.

In addition to the protests from the fans, there was much negativity throughout the press and the wider footballing community. Questions were asked in Parliament, and one enterprising fan secured a debate at the Liberal Democrat party conference. As for the villainy on the part of the club's owners, there is a long list that could go in here, but perhaps the most emblematic incident came when club chairman Charles Koppel was recorded telling a meeting of Merton residents that football supporters weren't really the kind of people you wanted present within a community. Generally speaking, throughout the split the owners of Wimbledon consistently defaulted to an assumed hierarchy, one which placed the broad category of 'football fans' beneath not just themselves but everybody else. Looking back, you get the impression that 'the fans' existed in the imagination of Wimbledon's owners only as a lumpen and undifferentiated mass, distinctly other and inherently inferior. It seems to have come as quite a shock that they turned out to be intelligent, varied, articulate, engaged, organised, capable, possessed of rich interior lives, and furious. And this attitude, which can be detected at various points throughout the history of English football, persists to this day. In May 2021, as the dust settled on the failed Super League, Alan Sugar told TalkSPORT that plans to involve fans at boardroom level were "Absolutely totally ridiculous." Football clubs need "people of knowledge who know what they're talking about." This is not a test that English football extends to anybody looking to buy a club, of course. That's a question of promised funds and very little else.

That opposition should harden as the prospect of the move became more and more realistic was of course inevitable. But one interesting consequence of the whole process, of the protests and of the working-through of arguments, was that the fans didn't just get angrier from the outside. Instead, they actively began to encroach on the operational territory of the club.

The most obvious example of this was the founding of the Dons Trust, which was launched in February 2002 at Wimbledon Theatre in front of more than 1,200 people, including local politicians and former players. Supporters' trusts are explicitly committed to acquiring or creating opportunities for fans to become involved in the running of their football club, and some English clubs have at times included trust representation on their boards. Such a collegiate approach couldn't have worked at Wimbledon in this particular moment: Koppel maintained throughout the process that the choices were Milton Keynes or liquidation. In the absence of any possibility for cooperation, then, the foundation of the trust amounted to a statement of intent — the club will be ours — and Lord Faulkner, a former director of the club, concluded that first meeting by calling for a new stadium in Wimbledon "at the heart of our local community".

A more unusual example of this assumption of operational duties came with the founding of *Yellow and Blue*, an alternative programme written and printed by Wimbledon fans. It is important to note, and not just for pedantic reasons, that *Yellow and Blue* was fan-produced but was not a fanzine. On the off-chance you're not clear on the distinction, the publication of a matchday programme for every home game is mandated by the FA. They are produced by the club, and typically they include official club announcements, notes from the chairperson or owner, a column from the manager, squad lists, fixtures and results, travel information, player interviews, and a lot of local advertising. Fans are often involved with their production as contributors and sometimes even editors, but they remain the official organ of the club.

Fanzines, by contrast, are giddily and fundamentally *un*official. Fans make them at their own expense and sell them under their own cognisance; as distinctive as the lark or the cuckoo is the cry of the fanzine seller: "No mate, it's not the programme". What they lack in official access to players and the club they make up for with the absolute freedom to write whatever takes the contributors' fancy. Accordingly, it is impossible to provide a comprehensive overview of what might be found in any given fanzine, but common themes include reviews and opinions on music, films and books; comic strips mocking rival clubs; a bottom-up approach to club history; gonzo match reports; a general sense of irreverence larded with mordant irony; and sharp criticism — often warranted, sometimes not — of players, management, and particularly club officials. Some are able to scoop interviews with former players, and many have contacts within the game and football media. But all remain defiantly and proudly outside the system.

The point to emphasise here is the clear delineation between the official and the unofficial: what is made by the club to fulfil an administrative function, and what is made by the fans to fulfil their desires to have a space of their own. It is a strict practical and conceptual divide, and it was thoroughly demolished by *Yellow and Blue*, which amounted to nothing less than a strategic capturing of enemy territory. This was explicit: the issue that accompanied Wimbledon's home game against Watford on 19 February 2002 states that this publication will be "far less irreverent" than the fanzines that have come before, and will "serve a wider audience and promote itself as a serious alternative to Pravda". That reference to Wimbledon's official programme demonstrates that the protest spirit was there throughout, and while the club organ was being used to press the case for the move to Milton Keynes, *Yellow and Blue* was pointedly opposed and on "a quest for truth". But it was also a functional programme, complete with squad lists, match previews, travel information, and so on. By the end of the season it was outselling the regular programme three to one, and copies were finding their way into the Wimbledon dressing room.

As well as seeking to supplant the official programme, Wimbledon's fans ended the 2001/02 season by improvising in the face of unanticipated player sales. Popular winger Kevin Cooper was sold to Wolverhampton Wanderers as the season wound down, but Wimbledon still had to visit Molineux. And so, after Wimbledon's travelling fans watched their side lose 1-0 to the team that had bought their best player, they presented Cooper with the Player of the Year award on the pitch. Such awards are often organised and presented by fans, or fans' representatives: what was unusual here was that Wimbledon FC were never told at any stage. The fans, through their supporters' association (WISA), had organised the presentation with the assistance of the staff at Wolves; with Koppel and the owners effectively absent, they had stepped into the administrative void. Cooper, for his part, was deeply moved:

> I'll be honest, the tears were streaming from my eyes. The emotion then … it's just so hard to describe. It's better than winning games and scoring goals. To be appreciated by the supporters of the club you have just left in such a way; I just don't think anything in football can better that. It was amazing.

One WISA board member at the time recalled the dominant attitude behind *Yellow and Blue*, the Player of the Year award, and other similar actions — such as the maintenance of the football in the community programmes through the Dons Trust — as being driven by a kind of emancipated curiosity: "Why can't we do X?". Apparently "It wasn't often that people came up with good answers to that."

There was a back and forth under way here, the actions of the club prompting a response from the fans, which in turn prompted another manoeuvre from the club, and so on: a dialectic that produced and reinforced division.[18] Consider the Official Wimbledon Fans Forum,

[18] Writing in the 1930s, American anthropologist Gregory Bateson developed a theory to describe how groups of people within a larger and apparently coherent group nevertheless generate conflict between themselves. He called it schismogenesis, "the creation of division", an excitingly dramatic word for an instinctively familiar process. Schismogenesis is what happens when the cumulative actions of individuals or groups serve to create "differentiation in the norms of individual behaviour": that is, they change how people behave. It is the process of "reactions of individuals to the reactions of other individuals" and, as it is reinforced through each cycle of reaction, the two parties grow apart. Unchecked, one party destroys or consumes the other; more often, at least by Bateson's account, other factors or processes act to check this before it reaches a crisis point, and the two parties continue to exist in a state of "dynamic equilibrium".

Of course, the two sides of this particular argument were by no means equally composed, whether in numbers or in their capacity for action. Bateson identified two distinct kinds of schismogenesis, symmetrical and complementary, and it is the latter that we might be able to apply to intra-club divisions such as that of Wimbledon. Complementary schismogenesis involves two groups that are fundamentally different in their behaviour and aspirations: their actions are "essentially dissimilar" but "mutually appropriate". Such is the case with Wimbledon, where both parties acted entirely in accordance with their own interests towards their own desired ends. The owners, having bought a football club on the incorrect understanding that it would shortly be moving to Dublin, and so to profitability, sought to find an alternative that would extricate them from the awkward, expensive oversight that Wimbledon required; they found, in Milton Keynes, a business-appropriate way out. As for the fans, return again to Stewart's words after the takeover was confirmed — "I just want to watch football" — and the unspoken but fundamental qualification: in Wimbledon, as Wimbledon. And so, two clubs: unprecedented, painful, and perfectly comprehensible in light of the actions and motivations of each of the parties involved.

set up by Koppel to validate his assertion that protestors were a noisy minority. This proved both provocation and inspiration: 29 of the 30 applicants for the seven seats allocated to fans were opposed to the move, and the single pro-move candidate finished last in the voting. As one of those elected recalls:

> The meetings that followed frequently descended into farce. [...] The 'extensive' study of sites investigated in London consisted of a map. The promised 'more detailed evidence' was never shown to us. In March Koppel said that he would happily sell the club for a pound but because of the club's financial plight he wouldn't have any takers. Sadly he declined my outstretched hand with a pound in it.

Through the 2001/02 season, as the club's owners worked to secure their move away from south London, a conceptual space opened up in anticipation of the real space that would soon

---

By Bateson's conception, complementary schismogenesis often takes the form of one party acting in an assertive fashion, the other responding in a submissive fashion, and each reinforcing the other: assertion bringing greater submission which, in turn, brings greater submission, and so on. If left unchecked, this ends in the breakdown of the social system. And it is certainly possible to conceive of the dynamics of 'the fans' vs. 'the club' as operating along submissive-assertive lines, not least because the terms of fans' interactions with the club are generally mediated by the club itself, which sets the ticket prices, controls access to the ground, employs stewards and liaises with the police, and so on. Further, it is 'the club', through the purchase and acquisition of players and coaching staff, that defines the nature of the team that actually plays the games. The fans' choices are, essentially, like it or lump it: they can pay the prices they are asked and watch the team they are given (so submitting and encouraging further assertion), or they can withdraw from active support and so from the process altogether. Many clubs have no formally designated space for fan involvement with a club's operations, and where they do exist such channels are often weak and sometimes ignored entirely. Protests are possible, and can be both striking and effective, but it remains relatively straightforward for club owners to ignore anything short of a full economic boycott, and full economic boycotts are exceptionally rare.

become available. And Wimbledon's fans moved to fill this space, so that by the time the final decision came in May 2002 they were already in possession of a large supporters' trust, they were producing a programme, they were looking after community initiatives, and they had anointed their player of the year. And the shape of the MK Dons was coming as well. Throughout the process, broad swathes of fans identified a fundamental wrongness with the whole business. Independent football magazine *When Saturday Comes* (WSC) railed against a "staggering ... hugely damaging" ruling that "destroyed two of the essential elements of the way British football has been organised: that clubs should be based in the area from which they draw their identity; and that progress through the leagues should be on merit". Protests from Tottenham, Luton and Charlton fans led to the cancellation of pre-season friendlies against the relocating club. And this sense of wrongness persists: WSC have since refused to ask MK Dons fans for season predictions, and plenty of my survey respondents recalled and reaffirmed their anger.

Franchise Football is Theft

Must admit my reply is also partly an emotional response based on distaste for MK Dons' 'franchise' concept which is poison to football culture as I understand it.

The process of contesting the move of the club that would eventually cease to exist served to shape the clubs that would emerge afterwards: on the one hand a coherent and united collective already performing a number of the functions of a football club; on the other an organisation that would soon slump into administration and then, on emergence, abandon most of the principles used to justify the move and settle into a still-lingering pariah status. Indeed, if you'll forgive a little theoretical glibness, we can loop back to Joe Kennedy's Marxist framing. Wimbledon's fans didn't just abandon the club, or have the club abandon them; in a small but significant way they began to reclaim the means of production.

PART 2:
Home and away

Chapter Four:
Milton Keynes: Satan's lay-by

For a lot of football fans there wasn't much about Wimbledon's proposed move that felt good or correct. But it was extremely fitting that the destination was to be Milton Keynes, a town that exists in England's national consciousness as a kind of floating punchline. The title of this chapter comes from the comedian Bill Bailey, the conclusion of a skit that pivots on the ridiculousness of going to see a heavy metal gig in Milton Keynes. The audience is left in no doubt as to which of heavy metal and Milton Keynes is the most ridiculous.[19] And if you've ever asked anybody where they come from and been told "Milton Keynes", the odds are good that this was quickly followed by "I know, I know. Roundabouts and concrete cows." It is a place that provokes its own reflexive apology.

The largest of the new towns built to provide housing in post-war Britain, Milton Keynes was formally designated in 1967 and constructed through the early 1970s. Practically speaking, the process of creating Milton Keynes involved taking a chunk of northern Buckinghamshire with access to the west coast mainline railroad, and filling in the space between and around a number of already existing towns and villages: Wolverton, Stony Stratford, Bletchley, Newport Pagnell, and a few others, including one for which the town is named. Perhaps the most well-known and

---

[19]   In any case, the *best* way to watch gigs at the MK Bowl is by pitching up on the scrubland outside. If by 'best' you mean 'cheapest' and by 'watch' you mean 'kind of hear, a bit, through the trees'.

notorious aspect of Milton Keynes' design is the grid system of main roads that divides the town into boroughs, each junction of which is joined by a roundabout. The roads are named but they are also coded — H for horizontal, V for vertical — and numbered. Though not quite as rigidly square as similar grid systems in the USA and elsewhere, this kind of superimposed top-down structure to a town or city is unusual in England, and is held by some in great suspicion.

This grid was underpinned by a grand, almost utopian vision. The idea was to avoid the rigid social delineation that had appeared in other new towns: each grid square would comprise its own self-contained borough containing schools, shops, and light industry; a place where, by its planners' vision, "workers, managers, vicars and doctors" would rub along together, freely, with "no fixed conception of how people ought to live". Cars would pass along the main grid roads while pedestrians and cyclists would pass under and over them, thanks to a network of 'redway' paths and underpasses that infiltrated the whole town. It was to be a town of villages, all quilted together, with the stitchwork hidden behind copious banks of trees and with a mighty shopping centre at its heart.

Almost since its foundation, Milton Keynes and the idea of Milton Keynes have been contested within British cultural and political discourse. Writing in the 1970s, Christopher Booker, one of the founders of *Private Eye*, recoiled in disgust at the sudden appearance in England of "the utterly depersonalised nightmare which haunted Aldous Huxley in *Brave New World*." Later, in the 1980s, Beryl Bainbridge retraced J.B. Priestley's *English Journey* for the BBC. Ending her journey with Milton Keynes, she declared that "If I had to describe the area in one sentence, I would say it was a series of motorways circled by endless roundabouts, with the houses hidden behind clumps of earth", and concludes that "if Milton Keynes had been in existence 50 years ago, Priestley would have made a detour around it."[20]

[20]   Later in the book, Bainbridge asks a Milton Keynes-based architect whether he likes Milton Keynes. He suggests that she think of it in

Or as one of my survey respondents put it: "Fuck Milton Keynes it's an awful place that's soulless."

The criticism has crossed political lines and shifted as the political conversation has shifted. As Patrick Barkham has noted in the *Guardian*, "The right attacked it in the 1970s for embodying the totalitarian planning of the welfare state; the left criticised it as a consumerist totem of Thatcherism. It has been cast as representative of the rootlessness of New Labour [and] as the doomed apotheosis of the fossil-fuel society." Perhaps, then, it is not just a floating punchline but a universal donor, the O-negative of English urban doomsaying. A place to be invoked whenever somebody needs to suggest that something — anything — has gone wrong with the process of building Britain as Britain should be built.

It was also, by the mid-'90s, home to a couple of hundred thousand people, and I was one of them. My family moved to Milton Keynes in January 1994, when I was 10 years old, after my mum got a job teaching French at a comprehensive in Wolverton, the north-west corner of the new town. I remember being excited: Milton Keynes had a multiscreen cinema inside a giant red pyramid, a fact that instantly rendered any place without a cinema-pyramid irrelevant. Even Egypt seemed diminished: sure, Khufu may have been proceeding to the afterlife with his slaves and his treasures, but he wasn't watching *The Lion King*. Before we moved we had been living in Hayes, out to the west of London near Heathrow, and Milton Keynes promised all the shimmer and shine of central London but without the hour or so on the Underground to get it.[21]

---

different terms: not whether it is likeable but whether it works. He goes on to claim that where previous towns and cities had been built around industry, this one was built around the credit card. Bainbridge finds this more convincing, at least until she sees "all those silly lamp-posts" and begins to "despise the place all over again."

[21] Another ritual: once the apology is out of the way, the next time somebody makes a crack about Milton Keynes to a former resident, that resident must in turn offer a defence. Some vague muttering about the quality of life, perhaps. And so, to observe the forms, I will say that broadly speaking I enjoyed growing up there, and while I've no particular

By happy accident, my early life in Milton Keynes amounted to a short investigation into the difference between the new parts of the new town, and the old. At first, we lived in Stacey Bushes, one of the new-build areas. Generally speaking, the streets within any given borough of Milton Keynes are named thematically: Oldbrook, for example, which used to have a community cricket ground on its central green, can boast Edrich Avenue, Trueman Place and Arlott Crescent, along with a long sweeping road called The Boundary.[22] To quote my grandfather, we were in Reggie Perrin country. Stacey Bushes' theming is a little more opaque, and the street names hark back to pleasantly old-fashioned fauna: Briar Hill, Myrtle Bank, Aldermead, and so on. We lived on a looping little road called Broomfield, and I went to Greenleys Middle School, an institution about which I remember very little except that the uniform policy, in relaxed fashion, suggested that pupils should wear something green. Accordingly, I turned up for my first day in a baggy, shapeless, toothpaste green pullover we'd manage to scrounge up from somewhere, only to find nobody else wearing anything green at all.

A few months later, perhaps to escape my shame, we moved to Wolverton and I moved schools again. By contrast to Stacey Bushes, Wolverton is *old*: it's mentioned in the Domesday Book, and though that village was deserted in the wake of enclosure, in the 19th century a point just southeast was chosen for the London-Birmingham railroad's locomotive repair shop. The Wolverton Works opened in 1838 and became famous, relatively speaking, for constructing and housing the carriages of the royal train, and the new town of its own time that grew up around the works has been called the first railway town in the world.

---

wish to return I know plenty of people that moved away for university or work but have since moved back. The pedestrian redway network is (or at least was) genuinely excellent, and if you had a free hour you could walk to the city centre from the edge of town without ever needing to cross a main road, the busy traffic mostly hidden although never quite hushed. Although I have since been told that actually walking into town was considered a bit odd. Why didn't we just drive?

[22]   There is, appallingly, no Brian Close.

Moving from Stacey Bushes to Wolverton in the summer of 1994, I do not know how much thought I gave to the difference between new and old Milton Keynes, but I do remember noticing the shifts in the ordinary stuff of daily life. The alleys weren't the smooth redways of the new town; they were damp and grey, edged with bricks and back gates rather than shrubbery. Our nearest park was a wide windy rec, not the small, sculpted spaces of Stacey Bushes; there were fewer but older trees. Our first, newer house had lower ceilings but better carpets, and was tucked away in an almost traffic-free cul-de-sac. The second was taller, thinner, older; the road outside was busier. It was a terraced house on a terraced street and it felt immediately familiar, of a piece with some of our earlier homes in Grantham, Newcastle and Middlesbrough. Other terraces in other towns.

Like a lot of England's small towns, and like a lot of England's railway works, Wolverton had a football team. Wolverton AFC were founded in 1887 and knocked around various Midlands amateur leagues for most of their existence, before joining the Isthmian League in the 1980s and then winding up in the early '90s. The club's most notable feature was the 100-capacity covered wooden grandstand, built in 1899 and claimed by some local historians as the oldest such structure in the country, by others as the oldest in the world.[23] It's still there, though it's not what it was: a near-faithful reconstruction looks out onto Wolverton Park and sees not a football pitch surrounded by a cycling track but a green space for new-build flats.

Beyond Wolverton, Milton Keynes and its constituent parts have had a few football teams over the years, though none have escaped the lower reaches of non-league. There is currently a Bletchley Park, and there has previously been a Bletchley Town and a Bletchley United. Newport Pagnell Town have been around since the '60s and currently play in the Spartan South Midlands League.

---

[23]   This means that for one tiny moment in time, just after the opening of Stadium MK, Milton Keynes held both the world's oldest and the world's newest places for watching football without getting rained on.

Wolverton's demise means that the oldest club in the area is Stony Stratford Town, founded in 1898. And — perhaps reflecting the town's ongoing and fruitless quest for city status — there have been two teams called Milton Keynes City, neither of which lasted long. The first was a rebrand of Bletchley Town, and played from 1974 until the mid-'80s. The second took over Wolverton AFC's ground in the late '90s but only lasted a few years, folding in 2003 when sponsorship dried up in the looming shadow of Wimbledon. Apparently they offered to sell the name to the incoming club, with the intention of resurrecting the name Wolverton AFC for themselves, but the consortium were at that point determined to keep 'Wimbledon' on the badge.

I lived in Milton Keynes until I was 18, then I moved to London in the summer of 2002, a year before the Dons headed up the other way. And yet I cannot, throughout that time, recall anybody having any interest in — mentioning, even — any of the various non-league sides that were pottering along around us. Football, proper football, was something that happened in other places. On the school playground and up the rec, in this town full of recently relocated families, everybody wore the colours of their family team. This meant mostly Arsenal or Tottenham, of course, with Euston just half an hour's train away, but there were other replica shirts as well: Manchester United and Liverpool, Coventry City and Sunderland, Aston Villa and Norwich City. We were a Manchester United household thanks to my stepdad — here a short pause for you to groan and roll your eyes — but as we didn't have Sky Sports, this mostly manifested in Cantona-esque collar-flipping and watching old United games on VHS. For a while, my favourite United goal was Lou Macari bouncing the ball off Jimmy Greenhoff's chest and past Ray Clemence to win the 1977 Cup final, six years and change before I was born.

As for live football, I particularly remember a couple of coach trips to the old Wembley to watch England U15s. Along with 30,000 others, I saw a young Michael Owen score the only goal of the game to beat Brazil; he got clattered near the edge of the box by Júlio

César, later of Inter and QPR, but rather than claim his penalty Owen got up and thumped the ball home. Such is the naivety of youth. Somewhere up the other end of the field, a young Wes Brown was marking a young Ronaldinho. I have a terrible memory for what happens on the pitch at football games I attend, but I vividly remember Wembley's heavy vastness; how 30,000 people, almost certainly the largest collection of people I'd ever seen, seemed swallowed and small. Age and import seemed to seep out of the place. The newer parts of Milton Keynes felt light, provisional, as though they were pinned in place; Wolverton and Wembley, in their different ways, felt stitched into the landscape.

As noted in chapter two, Milton Keynes was within reasonable reach of a fair few league clubs. The X5 bus ran from Milton Keynes through Buckingham, where I went to the grammar school, and onto Oxford, and for a couple of months towards the end of the 98/99 season I was a regular at the Manor Ground to watch Joey Beauchamp and colleagues get relegated from Division One. This included a 5-0 win over Stockport County on the last day of the season that, with the assistance of too much warm Fosters, made for a heady induction into the futile delirium that football does so well. Oxford needed a big win and friendly results elsewhere, and at half-time it became clear that only Oxford were doing their part. Cue wild, almost sarcastic celebrations for the rest of the game.

But the fact remains that Pete Winkelman, for all his unctuousness, had the germ of a point. Around the turn of the millennium, by England's standards, Milton Keynes was an unusually large cluster of humanity not to have a professional football club to call its own.

The socially acceptable, football-appropriate way to solve that problem would have been for Winkelman and his consortium to buy into one or other of the local non-league sides and begin the slow march up the leagues. This is a well-worn path, and there would have been grumbling about moneybags owners buying progress, but those rarely threaten to invite the kind of existential contempt that the Dons continue to attract. When it comes to the national conversation, non-league grumbles are quiet grumbles. And it is of course possible for a club to move from non-league to the very pinnacle of the English game: Wimbledon stand as proof of that.

But that would have been expensive, it would have taken time, it would have been hard going and, perhaps most importantly of all, it might not have worked. The consortium needed a stadium to get their superstores through the planning process, and nobody was going to sign off on a 30,000-seat ground for Milton Keynes City in the hope that they might be able to half-fill it in 20 years' time. The point of buying Wimbledon was that the work had already happened, as it were, off-site.

Historian Lauren Pikó has written extensively on Milton Keynes and its unusual place in the English imagination. Noting that Milton Keynes is "widely reviled in British media and popular culture", Pikó identifies this revulsion as being motivated, in part, by disquiet at Milton Keynes' newness. The town is "a deliberate and disastrous interruption of an idealised flow of incremental, osmotic landscape change", and the consequence of this interruption is a "drought of meaning" about the place.

How frequently any given part of England has actually been shaped by incremental or osmotic landscape change is of course up for debate: the first iteration of Wolverton was destroyed by enclosure, while the second was summoned into being by industrial necessity, and the latter in particular must have been relatively sudden. But Pikó is surely correct to say that this is the *idealised* understanding of how England became and becomes England: if there must be change, then let the change be so imperceptible as to be almost undetectable. A couple of counties over from Milton Keynes is Rupert Brooke's Grantchester, where the poet can lie "Day long and watch the Cambridge sky,/ And, flower-lulled in sleepy grass,/ Hear the cool lapse of hours pass,/ Until the centuries blend and blur". Or until somebody drops a roundabout on top of him.

There is a parallel here with the typical, idealised process of developing a football club. Incremental change is baked into the pyramid: do well, move up a division; do well again, go up again. Fail, and drop down. Bring in a new player here, another there;

let the old ones go. It is notable that as recent years have brought a faster turnover of players and managers, this has been matched by growing disquiet at the general chaos and lack of patience that typifies modern football. And while it would not have met with the same broad opprobrium as the move, folding and reforming as Wimbledon Town would also have constituted a rupture; less violent, perhaps, but still jarring.

The appropriate footballing cliché for a rise through the divisions such as Wimbledon's is *meteoric*, despite the apparent contradiction in terms of up and down. And meteors, though spectacular and unusual, are natural phenomena. If a meteoroid crashed through your window one day, you might marvel at the odds or bemoan your ruined carpet, but you would understand, broadly if not precisely, the processes that brought it there. An object, moving through space, encountering the tiny part of a much larger object that you happen to call home. By contrast, if a lump of space rock simply appeared in your house one day, without leaving an impact crater or an obvious path, that would be considerably more disturbing. One would be remarkable, the other inexplicable and troubling, despite the fact of the matter being the same: there's a big rock in front of the television.

Just as Milton Keynes can be understood as the irruption, physical and conceptual, of an upstart town into the idealised flow of the English landscape, so we can see how MK Dons compound this offence: a disruptive presence within the conceptual geography of English football; an oddity within an oddity. As such, it has utility, even and perhaps especially for those that despise it the most. Pikó has suggested that Milton Keynes stands as an "organising symbol to characterise all those values, aesthetics, and ideologies which are also seen as outside of ideal national norms". The same can surely be said of the town's football team.

***

The move was already in the air by the time I left Milton Keynes to go to university, but I recall very little anticipation or excitement about Wimbledon's arrival; at least, not among people around my age. Asking around some 16 years after the fact, the overriding memory among friends, and friends of friends, was that the club's owners were looking past older teenagers and younger adults, and focusing on families. Tickets for children were heavily subsidised — kids for a quid, and so on — and generous family packages were available. I wondered in chapter two how Wimbledon's owners imagined they might persuade football fans living in Milton Keynes to abandon their current allegiance and opt for the Dons, and here is the answer. A 25-year-old Arsenal fan with no family to look after isn't going to give up their Saturday afternoons in north London, but a 40-year-old Arsenal fan with two kids might be persuaded by something cheaper and more local. Those children then become MK Dons fans and the club begins to work itself into place.

It is frustratingly difficult to find any detailed record of how the people of Milton Keynes, broadly considered, felt about the acquisition at the time it was unfolding. Both Winkelman and Wimbledon's owners focused heavily on the projected interest — there are lots of people living here, and we know that a lot of them like football — and if they did carry out any targeted polling or focused research at the time, they don't appear to have been interested in sharing the results. Local councillors and Milton Keynes' two MPs were all publicly in favour, which at least suggests that the idea wasn't obvious electoral poison. In August 2001, local paper the *Sunday Citizen* went out to ask Milton Keynes shoppers what they thought of their incoming club and found that a "warm welcome" would be waiting, with just a couple of naysayers worried about drunkenness and hooliganism. One concerned aesthete also felt Wimbledon's "kick-and-run style" would reflect badly on the town.

In August 2002, *WSC* printed two letters from Milton Keynes residents. The first, from a Northampton Town regular, dismissed Milton Keynes' claim to being the largest football-less conurbation in Europe as "spurious and irrelevant". The second railed against the boosterish tone of the local press coverage and asked: "We are told this a fantastic opportunity – for who exactly?":

> I don't support Wimbledon, won't get any corporate tickets and don't have a small business selling burgers. There are many hotel and leisure complexes in the city – we don't need another one. But more importantly, why should we 'get behind' the consortium and the club? ... we don't know who they are. This is just another business venture. The fact that it happens to be football is neither here nor there for us. Are they really naive enough to think that Milton Keynes residents will start supporting Wimbledon because it is geographically close? Get behind your local club, they are saying – but it's not really our local club, is it? It's someone else's.

Ahead of Wimbledon's first game at the National Hockey Stadium, the club's temporary home for their first four seasons in Milton Keynes, Winkelman reiterated his belief that the people of Milton Keynes were waiting in anticipation for the club to arrive. He felt that the club's story would find a sympathetic ear since, "like Wimbledon, most of the people who live here came from London and they moved for economic reasons; they left family and friends and their roots to start a new life here. I think they will look at the club and say, 'Great, they're like us'." A *Financial Times* report from around the same time doesn't quite bear out his optimism. Tom O'Sullivan found that "it would be wrong to say there was universal indifference" but quoted one local as typical of those he canvassed. "I think they could have advertised more. There is no sign that Wimbledon is coming. Anyway, I'm a Tottenham fan."

I spoke to one MK Dons fan who attended quite a few of the early games, and they recalled "quite a buzz around the city". But they went on to say that MK Dons remain the second team of many locals, and attendances have declined "with very few good seasons in recent years". As for the matchday itself, they report "very little atmosphere with the away fans often louder than the c.50 MK Dons fans that actually sing". Also, "the stadium is far too big".

Of course, somebody buying a ticket to see their second team pays the same at the turnstile as somebody with MLTN KYNS tattooed on their knuckles; they may not spend as much in the club shop. And attendances increasing or declining in accordance with form and opposition is commonplace for almost all football teams up and down the pyramid. But if Winkelman was right that Milton Keynes was craving top-flight football, then the town will still be hungry: the Dons haven't finished higher than 23rd in the Championship. Attendances for that Championship season averaged around 13,000; for their campaigns in Leagues One and Two, they have tended to end up somewhere between 8,000 and 10,000.

Those football fans outside Milton Keynes that have a good word to say about the Dons will generally reserve that word for the club's engagement with the youth of Milton Keynes. Kids that were too young to remember the move happening are now old enough to attend matches on their own initiative, and prices for young people have been kept low. Another local resident (though not a Dons fan) told me that a number of his friends that support the big north London teams now take their children along to Stadium MK as "a good way for the future generations to become invested in the team and see local heroes". The club's work with local schools and youth programmes is highly regarded, and so too is the academy: the club has produced a number of players that have gone on to play in the Championship and the Premier League, most notably England international Dele Alli. If there was a certain amount of hot air inflating the early stages of Winkelman's strategy, the second stage appears to have had more substance.

Chapter Five:
Continuity/Discontinuity

If much of the perceived wrongness of Milton Keynes and its football club comes from a sense of interruption, then the counterpoint to that should be a high value placed on a sense of continuity. Consider this, from historian David Kynaston's *Shots in the Dark*, a diary of supporting Aldershot Town through the 2016/17 season. Here, Kynaston is completing a supporters' survey on their website:

> One of the questions asks, 'How important are the following to your enjoyment of a match day?' Here are my answers, with 5 as the highest possible:
>
> - Atmosphere — 4
> - Quality of football — 3
> - Catering — 2
> - Facilities — 3 (would once have been 2 or even 1, but I'm getting old)
> - Other entertainment — 1
> - Comfort — 2
>
> The factors, of course, that would get my 5 are continuity of ground & of colours — but they weren't on offer.

It is perhaps unusual to see "continuity" presented along with atmosphere, catering, and so on, as a component part of the matchday experience. But it makes immediate sense: after all, a change in kit or in ground isn't just a disjunction with the past. It is also an immediate, affective shift. It alters the experience of watching a football club in ways that might seem abstractly trivial but have so far been fundamental to the experience of what you have watched, and where you have watched it. The trivial, repeated often enough, becomes the appropriate state of things.

When Bobby Robson's imagined child first climbed those steps and looked at that football pitch, they were affected by what they saw: so affected, in fact, that they fell in love. There is a strong sensory rush that comes with visiting a football ground for the first time — here's Dave Roberts, from *The Bromley Boys*, on his first trip to Hayes Lane:

> I loved the smell of liniment drifting up from the dressing rooms beneath the stand, blending with the harsh cigarette smoke. I marvelled at the sound of the crowd ... I had fallen in love with everything about them, from the colours of white and royal blue to the spacious stadium.

And in addition to the immediate sensory reports — the colours, the smells — there is also another effect that comes with catching sight of many football grounds for the first time: an almost overwhelming historicity. The whole scene is freighted with the years the club has existed and the events those years have borne. In that instant of first encounter, an old football ground appears both historically authentic and authentically historic: this is a place that has seen things, you realise, and at the same time, this is a place that *looks* as if it has seen things. Old football grounds, even the well-maintained ones, look lived in. They feel lived in.

And of course they *are* lived in, in the sense that people willingly and gladly — if not always happily — create and pass their lives here. The second thing that Bobby Robson's imagined child will see, once they have absorbed the great greenness of the pitch, will be groups of people going through their pre-game routines: greeting friends, nodding at acquaintances, picking up a fanzine, hanging a banner. Laughing, joking, and singing, just as they did last week; just as those before them laughed, joked, and sang. To arrive at an older football ground for the first time is to be confronted with — affected by — the realisation that what is new for you is old, perhaps generations old; that you are entering into a way of being that stretches back before you and, all being well, will stretch out long past you as well. Harry Pearson puts it nicely, in an interview with *The Athletic*:

> I remember being in the Fulwell End at Roker Park, in the Holgate End at Ayresome Park, with huge affection, probably because I was young. It's partly that but you also had a connection with the past. You knew what you were experiencing there was what your grandad experienced. There was a commonality. Part of football was to feel that continuum of history.

It is worth taking a moment to look more closely at the importance of continuity of ground, not least since such concerns feature so heavily in the story of Wimbledon: their evacuation from Plough Lane and tenancy at Selhurst Park; the use of MK Dons' new stadium to anchor the construction of an Asda and an Ikea; AFC Wimbledon's purchase of Kingsmeadow from Kingstonian, which they then controversially sold on to Chelsea; and AFC's construction of a new ground just yards from the original site of Plough Lane. But again, while Wimbledon's problems may have been taken to extreme ends, they are not the only club to have ended up departing their long-cherished — or at least, long-affectionately-tolerated-and-at-times-enjoyed — traditional home.

In the first 10 years after the second world war, three all-new football grounds were built for professional teams: Hull City moved to Boothferry Park in 1946, Port Vale to Port Vale Park in 1950, and Southend to Roots Hall in 1955. For the next 33 years, England's football clubs would stay where they were; though, of course, where they were changed around them, as clubs installed floodlights, opened new stands, added private boxes. Up to this point, English football grounds had generally been built with four separate stands, each of which was improved or altered one at a time, meaning that over the decades each stadium didn't just age but acquired an architectural idiosyncrasy and character all its own. Admittedly, much of that character in this period was determined not by improvements, but the opposite: attendances were generally declining, crowd violence was rising, and many clubs dodged the question of required improvements by closing off the more decrepit areas of the grounds or simply not doing the work. The state of England's football grounds became a question not just of shabbiness and character but of dangerous neglect.

Both the Valley Parade fire in 1985 and the Hillsborough disaster in 1989 led to investigations and legislation to improve grounds, and while the post-Hillsborough Taylor Report is noted for mandating all-seater stadiums in the top two divisions, the first club to move in a generation did so a couple of years beforehand. Scunthorpe United, unable to bring the Old Showground (opened 1899) up to post-Bradford safety standards, moved to Glanford Park in 1988. Then, in 1990, Walsall moved from Fellows Park (1896) to the Bescot Stadium. More than thirty clubs have since moved to all-new grounds, most recently Brentford, who left Griffin Park — opened 1904 and famous for having a pub at each corner — for the Brentford Community Stadium in August 2020. That's a lot of disrupted continuity.

Each ground move was different, of course, yet there were identifiable tendencies: towards cheaper land out on the edges of towns; towards identikit bowl-like stadia, built with accompanying retail parks or hotels. And there was a common thread of response, too; a sense that old homes were being lost, while the new places didn't feel like any kind of home at all. Ffion Thomas has labelled such moves "exurbanisation": the abrupt removal of a football club from the urban context in which it has grown, with negative consequences from the fans' point of view.

> Prevailing trends in both the form and location of new stadia in England have frequently contributed to a sense of placelessness. What has often in the post Taylor Report period been an economic-based prioritisation of efficiency and rationality in stadium architecture and design due to the availability of time, location and budget has made many new-build football stadiums seem almost indistinguishable and exchangeable.

Perhaps the high-profile move of recent years was that of Arsenal, who in 2006 left Highbury, their home of nearly a century, and moved to the newly-built Emirates stadium, at Ashburton Grove, just a short walk down the road. As such, they provide a large-scale test case as to what can happen when a club's continuity of ground is disrupted. Early reports from fans attending the Emirates tended to agree that it was very impressive in terms of facilities, but it was not, in some fundamental and important sense, home. There is a tendency in modern stadium design to trend towards a kind of interchangeably smooth experience: the Emirates feels very much of a piece with, for example, the new Wembley stadium, which opened the following year.[24] Indeed, Wembley is perhaps the apotheosis of this school of stadium construction: with its shining glass front, escalators, champagne bar, and pervasive corporate sheen, it resembles nothing so much as an airport.

This calls to mind Marc Augé's theory of 'non-places': locations such as airports, shopping malls and hotel rooms, in which human beings are rendered transient and atomised. These are spaces for moving through and consuming within, to which an individual has only a contractual relationship: passenger, driver, purchaser, and so on. Augé contrasts the non-place with anthropological places, which are, or are intended to be by the people that occupy them, places "of identity, of relations and of history". But a football crowd, even one going to a friendly in a half-full and fully corporate Wembley, would seem to fulfil those criteria.

Instead we might tweak the concept a little and call these new, high-end, modern stadiums *now*-places. That is, while they are places in which identity and relationships can flourish, they are designed to resist the *appearance* of history, to obviate the processes by which football crowds and clubs have traditionally inscribed and created themselves over time in their home grounds. Their shiny glass fronts do not age or degrade in the same way as brick or concrete; their designs are carefully managed and show none of the

---

[24]   In fact, both the Emirates and Wembley, along with Tottenham's new stadium and Stadium MK, were designed by the same firm, Populous.

kinks and oddities of grounds that have been slowly expanded over time; their pitches — even Wembley's, after a problematic start — are well maintained, free from slope or strange narrowness, and playable all through the year; and after every game, an army of ground staff appear to reset the whole thing. The stands of both the Emirates and Wembley are integrated into one broad uninterrupted circular sweep of seats; quadrants have replaced stands. Every time a fan arrives at a game they arrive at a brand new stadium, restored to factory settings, that does not suggest or allow a history that can be inhabited.[25] Indeed, they are almost anti-historic: they wipe clean. The place itself carries nothing forward and shows nothing backward. As Augé puts it of non-places: "What reigns there is actuality, the urgency of the present moment."

This is of course a design feature for a stadium like Wembley, which has no resident club and instead hosts a sequence of one-off football matches, concerts, and other large events, each isolated from the last. A Bobby Moore statue, a frieze of historic moments: things happened here, you might remember them, that will do. Up goes the arch, it can be any colour you like. But for a club like Arsenal, the move to a new stadium affected both the fans and, so it seemed, the team's results as well. So to counter this sense of unbelonging, to speed along the process of homemaking, Arsenal's owners implemented a process that they called *Arsenalification*.[26] Rather like a young child's assault on the walls of their bedroom, every spare inch of bare space at the Emirates was covered in Arsenal symbolism. A broad mural called *The Spirit of Highbury* depicts every player and manager to have represented the club at their former home. Statues of Arsenal heroes have been installed,

[25] There have also been complaints regarding the atmosphere at many new stadiums — I discuss this in chapter eight.

[26] Cognisant of their neighbour's troubles, Tottenham's new stadium came pre-Spursified — 'a bowl with a soul' — and includes a scaled-up replica of the cast-iron cockerel that sat on top of White Hart Lane. The architects faithfully reproduced every scratch, dent, and bullet-mark of the original: a new object, artificially aged-up to suggest the lived-in authenticity of the old.

pedestrian bridges christened in their honour. The quadrants of the stadium were renamed to match the stands left behind at Highbury, and a clock returned to the new Clock End. White seats were installed to pick out a cannon against the red of the stands, and banners were added to the tiers between the seats. And most striking of all: the stadium is wrapped in giant depictions of Arsenal players from throughout the club's history, arms around one another's shoulders, all turned inwards, as if gazing down on the pitch below.[27]

Almost all of this Arsenalification was and remains deliberately, consciously, almost aggressively *historical*, even as none of it is historic: it is about history, it is not of that history. The Clock End's clock is a larger facsimile of that which kept time at Highbury. The giants wrapped around the stadium are all dressed in their period-appropriate kit: Ted Drake in the baggy shirt and shorts of the '30s, alongside David Rocastle in '80s long-sleeves and short shorts. But both players were painted in the '00s. The effect is not, therefore, to reproduce the historical feeling of Highbury — the Emirates' own historical feeling will only come, if it can come at all, with the slow passage of time and of generations — but instead to point to it, to acknowledge it; in some sense to summon it.[28]

---

[27] This question of history still weighs heavily on Arsenal even after the process of Arsenalification has slowed. The club's 2020-21 third kit was white with spattered red lines on the diagonal: intended to evoke the famous marbled halls of Highbury, but also bringing along suggestions of raspberry ripple ice-cream or white bathroom tiles following an energetic murder. The launch video took the viewer into Highbury and showed us Arsenal players as mediaeval and Renaissance portraits. The camera lingered for a moment on the white marble form of Michelangelo's David Seaman, before 'discovering' Arsenal's badge — the new version, from 2002 — carved into ancient rock. History, or at least gestures towards history, are an important selling point, even where they tip over into a kind of desperation.

[28] To speak of Highbury as an unchanging ground is of course inaccurate: most of Archibald Leitch's original stadium was replaced in the 1930s, the Clock End was redeveloped in 1989, and the North Bank was entirely renovated in the early '90s, during which time Arsenal played in a three-

As Thomas puts it, this is not history but heritage. There was a history, once, somewhere else, and it was ours, and it looked a bit like this. She notes, too, that it seems to work: that on the whole fans report happiness with the effort and greater affection for the ground that emerges. Perhaps this is the best that can be hoped for from the early decades of a new ground: that with enough focused, decorative effort it can establish a productive, parasitic relationship with the old demolished space. That it can reach into the past and bring through the shades of those who came before, to remind you that somebody once did something beautiful and important somewhere else, but wearing a similar jersey. And what else have the ghosts of Highbury to do with their time, after all? Still turning out for the club, still pulling in the crowds, even after their death.

It will be interesting to see how AFC Wimbledon fans take to their new home at Plough Lane. Though not as grand as the Emirates, it will still be a new stadium, box-fresh, without any of the sense of history that seeps from the stained concrete, worn brickwork, and layered paint of older grounds. The original Plough Lane was small, cramped, knackered: 'a dump, but *our* dump'. The new version is a tidy, trim, perfect little ground, with housing and a squash club. But where the Emirates was built as a result of commercial pressure — Highbury couldn't support a crowd large enough to match Arsenal's ambitions — AFC's new Plough Lane represents not so much a disjunction as a reconnection. The disjunction came when they moved to Selhurst Park, then Kingsmeadow; now, a generation later, they are returning to a place just 200 yards from the first Plough Lane.

Perhaps a better comparison is with Brighton & Hove Albion, who were without a stadium for 14 years before moving into their new ground in Falmer on the edge of the South Downs. Ahead of the opening of the ground in 2011, Brighton commissioned local artists to provide much of the internal decoration: the resulting pieces marked not only the history of the club but also the time

sided stadium closed off with a mural. Nevertheless, the continuity of place remained, even as the place was reworked.

spent without a home, integrating the club's journey into the mark of its completion. For AFC, perhaps, the very location will do more than the club museum or fan zone: one fan, interviewed by the Guardian, described experiencing "some kind of flashback" on visiting the new site. "In the old days, I used to get the train to Haydons Road and go to a sweet shop before matches. We also used to spend quite a lot of time at the dog track and go banger racing there as well on Saturday nights, which is where the new ground is. It's all quite surreal." In August 2020, ahead of the opening of their new ground — fan-less, sadly, thanks to the pandemic — AFC Wimbledon released a series of short videos entitled 'Back to Plough Lane', which featured players, volunteers, and fans old and young reflecting on their upcoming new ground. Nick, a match-day volunteer with 'Not In The Wider Interests Of Football' tattooed down his right forearm in gothic strip, put it explicitly: "It's full circle. We're going back home. We've been displaced ... We're going back to our community, we're slotting back in."

* * *

As noted in the introduction, most of this book should in theory apply just as readily to women's football as to the men's game: the practice of being a fan of either is fundamentally alike.[29] However, the complicated and at times enraging history of the women's game in England means that the structures and context in which most men's teams have developed — having a ground, being able to visit that ground regularly — have rarely been in place for the women's game.

Women in England have been playing organised football for almost as long as men: the British Ladies Football Club was founded in 1895, and one-off games have been traced back to at least 1881. But the emergence of women's football as a spectator sport really began during the first world war: as women moved into industrial workplaces — munitions factories, light engineering, food production — they began to form works teams, and then competitive

---

[29]   Although football crowds do remain predominantly male: more on this in chapter nine.

networks between those teams. The most famous of these teams, Dick, Kerr Ladies, played a number of charity exhibition matches throughout the war and immediately after in front of large paying crowds, including over 50,000 at Goodison Park. These games took place with the blessing of the Football Association: Jean Williams, author of *A Game for Rough Girls?*, has suggested that the FA were keen to allow these immensely popular games to take place in order to claw back a little credibility after their widely criticised decision to keep the men's league programme running during the early years of the war.

However, a few years after the war ended, the FA reversed their position. In December 1921 they declared that football was unsuitable for women, and banned women's teams from using the pitch of any club affiliated either to the FA or to the Football League; that is to say, the vast majority of the dedicated football pitches in the country. Looking back it is hard to see this decision as anything other than a grotesque act of institutional misogyny, motivated by the desire to keep organised football a masculine space. It has been suggested that since the crowds watching the women's game were mostly men, sometimes in larger numbers than men's games, the League and the FA were worried for their own attendances. Of course, the FA could hardly say as much at the time. Instead, the resolution of 1921 read:

> Complaints having been made as to football being played by women, the council feel impelled to express their strong opinion that the game of football is quite unsuitable for females and ought not to have been encouraged. Complaints have also been made as to the conditions under which some of these games have been arranged and played, and the appropriation of receipts to other than charitable objects. The council are further of the opinion that an excessive proportion of the receipts are absorbed in expenses and an inadequate percentage devoted to charitable objects. For these reasons the council request clubs belonging to the association to refuse the use of their grounds for such matches.

With respect to the allegations of financial impropriety, Gail Newsham, historian of Dick, Kerr, has acknowledged that across the period immediately before the ban there is money unaccounted for, though she notes that "any irregularities certainly had nothing to do with the ladies". In any case, were such allegations to be proven, the fault and the fix would surely both be matters of administration. (The administrators of most of the women's teams of the time were men.) As for the idea that football was 'unsuitable' for women, this was greeted with disdain by the players but did find some support within the medical profession. Newsham quotes a Dr. Mary Scharlieb, of Harley Street: "I consider [football] a most unsuitable game, too much for a woman's physical frame." It appears the women that had been playing the game for years and would continue to do so did not factor into her diagnosis.

The ban stayed in force for 50 years. Initial attempts to found a Ladies Football Association foundered, and it proved difficult to establish local competitive leagues. A number of the larger teams that had emerged from the war, including Dick, Kerr, maintained their existence through the following decades, playing exhibitions and charity matches both within the UK and abroad. But as a spectator sport, the women's game was institutionally nomadic throughout those five decades.

Football as a participation sport for women continued to grow, however, and four years after Dick, Kerr folded in 1965, the Women's Football Association was formed. Two years later the FA ban was lifted. In 1971, Southampton Women's FC won the first Mitre Challenge Trophy, which would soon be renamed the Women's FA Cup. Attendances have trended upwards from this point: the first finals drew crowds in the low thousands, and the venue for the final changed every year or so until as recently as 2014. Now in place at Wembley, the most recent final (with fans permitted) drew a crowd of more than 43,000.

But while the appetite for women's football survived the FA's ban, if we are to conceive of the identity of a football club as something created through regular, repeated interested attendance of fans, something that is intimately tethered to a specific community and develops within a particular space, then it is sobering to think how difficult it must have been to build such an identity over 50 years of peripatetic existence. Doncaster Belles, for years the most famous name in English women's football, played at a number of different grounds from season to season. In the early '90s, they became the first women's team to play regularly in a professional stadium, briefly ground-sharing at Doncaster Rovers' Belle Vue, but they often had their games postponed at short notice in order to protect the pitch for the men's team. Club officials have speculated that this unpredictability cost them a significant amount of support.

Through the years of the ban and for at least a couple of decades afterwards, the location and practice of organised, semi-professional women's football was an ad hoc, almost improvised thing, to be fitted around the spaces utilised by the men's game. Many clubs lacked a fixed, long-term geographical presence in the communities they purported to represent, and so the process of establishing continuity, of fans creating the clubs as clubs, could only take place in highly adverse conditions. Kynaston believes that continuity of ground is the most important part of his Aldershot experience; even in 2021, very few of the women's teams in England, even the richest, have their own exclusive ground. Jean Williams again: "A defining feature of women's football is that it continues to be characterised by a struggle for space in the broadest sense."

The foundation of the Women's Super League in 2010 as a fully professional competition has at the very least been successful in establishing a greater presence for the women's game in the wider footballing consciousness; so, too, the recent strong showings of England women's national team. The FA, which incorporated the WFA in 1993, has pursued a policy of encouraging women's and men's teams from the same area to affiliate; other clubs, most notably Manchester United, have established women's teams under the same banner and badge as the men. The process of professionalisation has not been uncontroversial: in 2013, Doncaster Belles were demoted from the top tier of the Women's Super League on the basis not of sporting performance but of licensing criteria; their place was taken by Manchester City. More recently, in April 2021, Leyton Orient cut ties with Leyton Orient Women's Football Club, denying them the right to use the name in future.

In the search for a space for a women's team to call their own, Chelsea's women's team have just moved into Kingsmeadow, taking ownership from AFC Wimbledon who had themselves bought the ground from Kingstonian. Whether this emerges in time as a club-nurturing home remains to be seen: though AFC outgrew the ground, it had certainly worked for Ks, who now find themselves displaced to Leatherhead.

* * *

Let us make a brief detour to Scotland, where the people of Glasgow have been conducting a multi-year experiment in club continuity. The precise details of Rangers' insolvency, liquidation, and subsequent reconstitution have been debated vigorously and passionately ever since it all happened in 2012, and in a spirit of space-saving and cowardice I will not be trying to sort it all out here. But I hope the following is an uncontroversial summary of what happened.

First, Rangers entered administration in February 2012 in the face of a £50m bill from HMRC following years of alleged tax avoidance. Second, the club then went into liquidation after HMRC rejected the administrators' proposed settlement. And third, the club's assets were bought by a new company that reformed the club. After failed attempts to join the Scottish Premier League and the Scottish First Division, Rangers eventually joined the Scottish Third Division, the fourth (and lowest) tier of the Scottish league system.

They weren't called Glasgow Town, but clearly reforming a team with (at the time) 54 titles and 33 cup wins was considered to be in the wider interests of Scottish football.

The situations are of course markedly different, not least because nobody was suggesting that Rangers solve their problems by decamping to Cumbernauld.[30] The interesting question for our purposes is that of continuity. Whether Rangers should be considered a new club — with just the one league title as of 2021, no cup wins, and no particular special status beyond that — has been a point of vigorous contention ever since, and will remain so long into the future, far past the extinction of the human race and the descent of the earth into the fiery heart of the sun. Again, this book won't sort it out. But while it is clear that the question of whether Rangers are a new club remains a live issue within Scotland, I think it's fair to suggest that the broad mass of football supporters beyond any partisan interest quickly concluded that, on balance, Rangers were still Rangers; that their recent history, while turbulent, did not amount to the emergence of an entirely new club.

Obviously the opinion of a neutral from the other side of the border is fundamentally an irrelevant opinion, but you've had four and a half chapters of those already so another won't hurt. As an opinion, it is based in part on the continuities of location, stadium, colours and so on, but mostly due to the apparent continuity of the fan base. To an outsider such as myself, it appears that Rangers fans have largely considered themselves to be supporting the same club through the closure, re-opening and subsequent promotions: that they have continued to consider this Rangers of a piece with that Rangers, whatever the moment-to-moment legal status. The celebrations of the 2020/21 title as the 55th have reinforced this impression. Obviously, there is a certain self-interest at play there: far more fun to call oneself a supporter of the most decorated team in Scotland than not, particularly since that title would otherwise pass to Celtic. But if Rangers fans still think Rangers are Rangers, who am I to tell them otherwise?

This sense of continuity is supported by a ruling from the UK's foremost authority on the power of symbols in the public realm, the Advertising Standards Authority. Following a 2013 advertising campaign that referred to Rangers — the newly reconstituted

---

[30]   Apart from anything else, Clyde FC might have been a little upset: they had moved from Glasgow to Cumbernauld in 1994.

Rangers — as Scotland's "most successful" football club, the ASA received more than 80 complaints alleging that this was misleading, since the club in question had only come into existence in 2012. The ASA initially found in favour of Rangers, then reiterated this decision after an appeal, noting that UEFA's rules allow for recognition of sporting continuity even where a club's corporate structure has changed. Further, the Scottish Football Association's definition of a football club can also refer to an entity "separate from the club's corporate owner". Rangers' case is also buttressed by the mythological implications of football's chosen terminology. The phoenix, when it dies and is reborn in fire, does not return as a new bird: it is the old bird, once dead and now alive.

* * *

— What's the shirt, mate?

— FC United, mate. People's club.

— I wouldn't wipe my arse on that, pal … Listen, pal, you run off and left us.

— They left me!

— Who left you? United? The most famous team in history? We've got over 300 million fans, and we left you?

— Yes.

— Told you this before, right. Bloke once said: leave your wife — you can change your wife, change your politics, change your religion. But never, never can you change your favourite football team.

And now a detour to Manchester. Of the various protest and phoenix clubs that have emerged in English football, FC United of Manchester are perhaps the most unusual, in that their formation was not prompted by either a geographical departure or a financial collapse. Manchester United continue to exist and continue to play their home games at Old Trafford. Though they are not quite the remorseless accumulators of silverware that they were under Alex Ferguson's management, they are still one of the strongest sides in the country, and while the Glazer family's takeover has left the club servicing a vast debt, the prospect of the business side of Manchester United collapsing remains a distant one.

The dialogue above comes from a pub scene in Ken Loach's film *Looking for Eric*, which follows a Manchester United-supporting postman as his life falls apart; in his desperation, he hallucinates a guardian angel in the form of Eric Cantona, who glowers charismatically while dispensing cryptic advice. But the FC United fan from the clip has not been left in any tangible sense; rather, the abandonment — "They left me!" — is a question of behaviour, conduct and function. FC United were formed in response to the takeover of Manchester United by the Glazer family in 2005. Before a friendly game against Leigh RMI in July of that year, a leaflet was distributed setting out the "seven core principles" of the new club:

1. The Board will be democratically elected by its members
2. Decisions taken by the membership will be decided on a one member, one vote basis
3. The club will develop strong links with the local community and strive to be accessible to all, discriminating against none
4. The club will endeavour to make admission prices as affordable as possible, to as wide a constituency as possible
5. The club will encourage young, local participation — playing and supporting — wherever possible
6. The Board will strive wherever possible to avoid outright commercialism
7. The club will remain a non-profit organisation

Each of these points amounts to a rebuke to what Manchester United had become in the eyes of the rebels and many others: unaccountable to its fans; divorced from its community; overpriced; over-commercialised; and focused, above all, on profit. We might even suggest that, taken altogether, it amounts to a case that Manchester United have in fact left Manchester: that the club, while remaining in the same geographical location, has deterritorialised, sloughing off its localised identity to become an untethered global presence. From emplaced club to abstract, heavily leveraged brand: all that was solid melts into Aeroflot.[31] As already mentioned, that removal of "Football Club" from the badge in 1998 stands as a harbinger of this moment, a blatant transition from football club to brand.

The Glazer takeover did not represent the arrival of these problems; rather, it amounted to a point of intensification that justified a departure. It was clear throughout that the takeover would be contingent on a leveraged buyout — one that raised the money through loans and then placed the debt generated onto the club — and the dissenting fans believed that this would necessitate a ramping up of United's commercial activities and the hiking of ticket prices, as well as the diversion of club income away from improving the team or lowering ticket prices and towards debt service and dividends. And indeed, United proved so good at finding new sponsorship streams to pay for the privilege of being owned by the Glazers that the man in charge of striking those deals, Ed Woodward, was soon placed in charge of footballing affairs as well. United's fans, meanwhile, have coined a word to describe the chaotic and often wasteful business in the years that have followed: Glazernomics. That the announcements of the Super League came with a statement from Joel Glazer attached was only a surprise because United's owners have tended not to say anything at all. Here were the big clubs all deterritorialising together, untethering themselves from the communities and contexts that built them. FCUM saw them coming years ago,

In FCUM's mini-manifesto, we again see the priority placed on the closeness of club, place, and community, here constituted not in terms of proximity but instead connection and access: the presence of the club in the community and the community in the club. The significance of this connection was literalised in December

---

[31]   Official carrier of Manchester United. Much of Manchester United's financial productivity under the Glazers has come thanks to an aggressive policy of seeking out unlikely-sounding commercial partnerships, and the club's website currently boasts about 50 such partners, regional and global, including a 'lubricant partner' , a 'vision partner', an 'electrical styling partner' and a 'mattress and pillow partner'.

2014 when FC United launched the 'buy a brick' campaign to boost the club's development fund. For £45, fans could have their name and message installed on a wall of FCUM's new ground Broadhurst Park in perpetuity.

At the time of writing, FC United are the largest fan-owned club in England. We should note, however, that among Manchester United fans opposition to the Glazer move was by no means unanimous, and the eventual rebels amounted to only a small fraction of that opposition. Some Manchester United fans were sympathetic, but didn't feel able to abandon their club; others were openly contemptuous of the whole endeavour. Alex Ferguson dismissed them as "sad" "attention seekers". In the absence of a literal absence, FC United present a purely normative case, set against the surety of elite football and the likelihood of trophies. But in any case, it would perhaps be a mistake to presume that FCUM was an evangelical endeavour, and many FCUM fans still follow the other club, albeit at a remove. Rather, as with Wimbledon, there came a point where those involved just wanted to watch football, on the terms they understood to be most important. As Rob Brady puts it in his history of the first year of the rebel club, *An Undividable Glow*:

> We don't know where we're going but we know what we are taking with us. Part of us will stay forever at Manchester United Football Club, it could be no other way. Part of us has gathered what we believe to be the soul and wrapped it in the softest of cotton and placed it gently into a treasure chest for its protection against hardship and arrogance, and deceit, and treachery, and slyness. And the lid was closed. For so many it could be no other way.

Chapter Six:
The f-word

If there is one point of overarching agreement in the whole sorry saga of Wimbledon's move, it is that the introduction of franchising into English football would be a bad thing. Indeed, as noted in chapter two, the commission were so desperate to reassure everybody that they *weren't* permitting franchising that they had to make a moral case for Milton Keynes: ultimately they could only allow this particular instance of franchising by loudly proclaiming that they weren't doing anything of the sort.

Franchising, as it applies to sports, is the practice of a team's owners moving that team from one city to another. In England it is almost entirely understood as 'a thing that happens in the USA', and as such is treated as both slightly peculiar and wholly contemptible. And this is very much of a part with a broader tendency in English football culture, which through the '90s and into the 21st century seemed to orient itself around the idea of the USA as a place in which they Do Football Wrong.

The most obvious example of this is the very word itself: 'football' vs. 'soccer'. The latter word has its origins in the slang-making habits of England's private schools and elite universities: chop off the end, stick an 'er' on it. Rugby football became 'rugger'; association football, with Procrustean brutality, lost both head and tail and became 'soccer'. The word made its way over the Atlantic just in time for the other American football, gridiron, to emerge from the college system, and so took up the work of distinguishing the two codes. But this was far from the only name for the game, and historian Robert Colls notes that in Britain, 'soccer' retained its upper-class character through the first half of the 20th century; by his reckoning, working-class kids preferred the various regional shortenings of football: "'futta', or 'footie', or 'futball'." In *It's Football, Not Soccer (And Vice Versa)*, Stefan Szymanski and Silke-Maria Weineck trace an upsurge in the word's popularity in the UK after the second world war. Indeed, for a while after the war the words seem to have been almost interchangeable: in 1973, Matt Busby published his autobiography under the title *Soccer at the Top: My Life in Football*. Hands across the Atlantic. However, by Szymanski and Weineck's analysis the use of the word in the UK declines sharply through the 1980s, a trend they attribute to "the rise of the sport — and its American word — in the US context". Their suspicion is that:

> It is precisely the game's growing popularity in the US that made its American name so much more unpopular in the UK. As long as those Yanks weren't a threat, nobody cared what they called the game — but now that they just might become an international force, they had to be defeated on the field and linguistically.

More recently, here's John Cleese from 2009, from his comedy documentary *The Art of Football from A to Z*:

> American football is played like a series of advertising jingles while soccer is played like jazz. And while we're on the subject, why do the Americans insist on calling it soccer? Why do they have such a problem calling it football? It's a game played with a ball that is struck with the foot. Hence: foot, ball. You see? Are you following this, America? The clue is in the title. It's not that difficult.

That clip doesn't end with him hitting a small Spanish midfielder with a frying pan, but it might as well do. Quite how seriously we should take such demonstrative disdain is not quite clear: with Cleese, as with England in general, it's increasingly hard to tell where the self-awareness ends and the self-righteousness begins. But even if we allow that he's in on the gag, the gag is still being made at somebody's expense: either the silly Americans with their silly words, or the silly Brits with their silly huffing and puffing.

The worry over vocabulary extends into the language of description and conversation. In 2002, the *Guardian*'s Scott Murray sprinkled his online minute-by-minute commentary of the USA's men's World Cup game against Mexico with parodic pseudo-Americanisms such as "Flag! Eddie Pope is yellow-marked for contact infringement" and "Mastroeni is put on report for a charging transgression". After 64 minutes, the USA doubled their lead, and Murray wrote:

> Two soccer points to no score! Eddie Lewis makes a cross-pitch play from the left zone, finding Landon Donovan alone in the danger area. He top-bodies the sphere into the score bag, and Mexico have a double-negative stat!

The force of the parody, and the willingness of the English to believe the worst of the USA's football coverage, was demonstrated when Gary Lineker read out this last quote on the BBC's World Cup coverage, apparently under the impression that he was sharing genuine commentary from the USA. Nearly 20 years later, the joke is still stumbling on, and has reached a kind of full-spectrum nadir with the parody Twitter account @usasoccerguy, which can boast more than 100,000 followers on Twitter ("An American slice of the soccer pie"), over 10,000 on Instagram ("Well respectified soccer expert"), and a website selling t-shirts: 'London Cannons', 'Felony Kick', and so on.[32]

---

[32]   By way of illustration, here is @usasoccerguy on Arsenal's elimination from the 2019-20 Europa League by Olympiakos (all spellings as in the original): "Obama Yang cries like a baby racoon that just saw its momma have her brains blown out by some guy who had had it with her stupid racoon ass messing up his garbage cans as the Soccer Cannons go lose 2-2 to Olympic Argos. Knotted at ones on aggregization at the end of regulization time, Yang inserted a presidential no bounce kick to put the Cannons ahead right before the end, only for them to go do some dumbass

Beyond the vocabulary sits a whole mass of strange American otherness, a mélange of purported offences to the sensibilities of 'proper football'. Half-remembered incidents from the glory days of the North American Soccer League and the early days of Major League Soccer — a bearded George Best, well past eponymity, walking round the Fort Lauderdale Strikers; penalty kicks that began like ice hockey free shots at the halfway line; kits with leather tassels running across the front — coalesce into a grand mass of supposed unseriousness, a sense that the beautiful game is being besmirched and belittled. Overpaid, oversexed and overdoing soccer. *Football*. This was all neatly satirised by Budweiser, that most American of beers, which has been sponsoring English football competitions and teams for decades.[33] In 2005, the company announced their status as official beer of the Premier League with a series of adverts proposing 'Soccertainment': one featured half-time monster truck rallies and 'added-time multiball'; another spoke to franchising directly, proposing a merger between the Manchester clubs and, in a surely deliberate nod to Wimbledon, moving a club away from the capital. "Does London need so many clubs? Let's send Arsenal to the Peak District. They need a good team." But after all that Yank ridiculousness, the adverts concluded with a reassertion of the natural order of things: "You do the football. We'll do the beer."

I do not propose to attempt to unpick the cultural neuroses of the British as they relate to their former colony turned superpower: that would be a much longer, very different book. But I think it's fair to suggest that the idea of the USA as a football-playing, football-*degrading* nation has often been deployed as a kind of rhetorical consolation. The ridiculousness 'over there' used to confirm the sensibleness 'over here', like a tutting neighbour peeping through the curtains at the party next door. Sure, they look like they're having fun. But they're not living right. That can't be healthy. And do they have to be so *loud*.

---

deefense at the other end of the field to let Argos insert what turned out to be the winner on the roadtrip goalshot rule."

[33]   At the time of writing, Budweiser are the official beer partners of the England senior men's team, the FA Cup and Wembley Stadium.

This used to come with a general layer of contempt for football as it is played on the other side of the Atlantic: ahead of the 2010 men's World Cup, after England were drawn into a group with Algeria, Slovenia and the USA, the Sun ran an acrostic on their front page: "E.A.S.Y." — the Y standing for 'Yanks'. It was, apparently, the "Best English Group Since The Beatles", though in the end England found it hard going. They drew 1-1 with the USA after a goalkeeping error, and then nil-nil with Algeria in one of the worst games of football of all time.[34] Though they beat Slovenia, they could only finish second in the group, behind the USA, which cued up a thrashing by Germany in the last-16.

As with the chortling over the funny words, this all feels exceedingly dated. MLS may not have promotion and relegation, and the title may be decided by playoff, but the days of the truly wacky rules innovations have long passed and the USA now plays the same game as everybody else.[35] Three of England's biggest clubs are wholly or majority owned by Americans — Manchester United, Liverpool, and Arsenal — and the Premier League's recent decision to eschew a main sponsor — no more Carling, no more Barclays; just 'Premier League' — echoes the assertive branding of the NFL. At a corporate level, the ideas are flowing in both directions. And in any case, it's very hard to maintain that the USA isn't doing football correctly when the USA women's national team is so remarkably dominant. Doing it differently, perhaps; so is everywhere else. But something must be going right somewhere.[36]

---

[34] This is not an exaggeration. It was a game so utterly goalless that a bird was able to take a nap in one of the goal nets.

[35] In fact, when it comes to changing the laws of football, 50% of the voting power belongs to FIFA while the other 50% belongs, by tradition or anachronism, to the football associations of the home nations. Changes require a three-quarter majority, meaning that if FIFA wants to change the rules of the games it oversees, it has to persuade two of England, Wales, Scotland and Northern Ireland to go along with it. Added-time multiball has no chance.

[36] The preeminence of USA's national women's team over England was reinforced in the 2019 World Cup, when the two sides met in the semi-

I mention all this to ground the discussion of franchising in a wider context of casual anti-Americanism, but also because I wish to pick out disquiet as to franchising from this wider tendency. The assertion that 'football' is somehow more correct than 'soccer' is partly an aesthetic argument, partly cultural paranoia. Franchising is a different thing altogether: a materially distinct method of organising the sport itself. And the nature of that difference is intimately related to the idea of a football club.

Another parallel with Milton Keynes emerges here. Much of the early disquiet with Milton Keynes in the late '60s and early '70s, as it passed through the planning stage and into the landscape, focused on the grid system, and particularly on the grid system's supposed inherent Americanness. Los Angeles in Buckinghamshire: a self-evidently ludicrous conjunction. The grid system was both futuristic and foreign, two powerful others. Lauren Pikó reads this coverage of Milton Keynes as connecting with a wider declinist narrative of Britain's changing place in the world, particularly in relation to its lost Empire.

> By presenting the grid system as a rationalising form associated with the cultural influence of a former colony, the English landscape was invoked as being subjected to the subsuming logic it had imposed forcefully elsewhere. The association of the grid with futurism rather than the past speaks to its association with frontier construction but also to the perceived newness of the inversion in power relations implied by American influence.

---

final and the USA emerged comfortable 2-1 winners. After scoring the decisive goal, Alex Morgan celebrated with a mimed sip from a cup of tea, her little finger extended in the proper English fashion. This was variously interpreted as a joke about the Boston Tea Party or a shot at England more generally as a nation of tea drinkers; Piers Morgan, no relation but always a useful dipstick by which to measure English pomposity, denounced this act of trans-Atlantic disrespect as a "declaration of war". Morgan herself later explained: "I feel like we didn't take an easy route through this tournament and 'that's the tea'." I was in the stadium, surrounded by delighted USA fans: it would have been hard to put together any sort of argument that they weren't doing it properly.

We might conclude something similar was motivating peculiar pieces like this one, by Sean Ingle in the *Guardian*, published as the arguments for and against Wimbledon's move were being made.

> Hold onto your Stetsons, stuff another hamburger down your throat, and start practising your Ricky (sic) Lake wave. Because if Wimbledon move to a new £50m super-stadium in Milton Keynes, the Americanisation of English football will be complete ... These days the economics, stupid, is all that matters.

Wimbledon's move, then, stands not just as something to be opposed on its own terms, but as the last stand in England's brave attempts to fend off re-colonisation. The club's owners were Norwegian, Charles Koppel came from South Africa and Pete Winkelman is as British as apple crumble ... but it was still the Americans.

All of this came roaring back into focus as the Super League appeared and then imploded. The American owners of Liverpool, Arsenal, and Manchester United were quickly identified as key drivers of the idea and during the protests American flags were burned outside the Emirates and Old Trafford. Despite the enthusiastic participation of Andrea Agnelli, chairman of Juventus and scion of one of Italy's foremost industrial families, and Florentino Pérez, president of Real Madrid, who made his money in Spanish civil engineering, the idea — particularly the closed league structure — was widely criticised as fundamentally American. It is true, of course, that the closed, relegation-free model of the Super League resembled MLS, the NFL, and so on; it is equally true that many American fans of European teams were drawn to their clubs precisely because of the un-American tangle of the pyramid and the jeopardy of relegation. Here, 'American' seems to be shorthand for cartel capitalism at its most vulgar, predatory and globalised.

One of the drivers behind Milton Keynes' grid system was a search for efficiency, as contrasted against the inefficiency of more traditional cities: as such, the grid was not just another way of doing things but an assertion of a *better* way, with the associated suggestion of inferiority in England's many more traditional elsewheres. And there is a similar echo of this search for efficiency

— in the distribution of football clubs rather than urban logistics — in the priorities, stated and implied, of the commission that sanctioned Wimbledon's move and the clique that plotted the Super League. The suggestion that Wimbledon could not continue in Wimbledon — that a club, in place since 1889, had not managed to develop adequate roots in the area in all that time — stands not just as a particular claim about a particular club but as an implicit criticism of the entire traditional model. If Wimbledon, with their hundred-year lifetime and their FA Cup win, couldn't even lay adequate claim to their place of origin, how could any troubled club? And surely, the key message from the Super League clubs — beyond the obvious surface reading of 'fuck you' — was that the traditional structures of football were simply inadequate for keeping them in the style to which they had become accustomed.

We should probably note here that while franchising is accepted and permitted within the closed professional leagues of the USA's major sports, it is by no means uncontroversial. A team that moves may not be cast into the abyss of non-existence in the manner of 'Franchise FC', but there may still be great and lasting opprobrium, not least from the place that has just lost its sports team. In basketball, the departure in 2008 of the Sonics to Oklahoma City is still mourned and bitterly resented within Seattle, where Sonics and retro SuperSonics shirts are available to buy in sport stores. As for baseball, Bernie Sanders, socialist senator for Vermont and occasional runner-up in Democrat presidential primaries, was a 16-year-old in Brooklyn in 1957 when the Dodgers were moved 4,000 miles west to Los Angeles; he later called this "a brutal act which impacted Brooklyn in a very significant way". His former chief of staff Huck Gutman has speculated to the *Guardian* that this was a formative experience, their first exposure to the fact that:

> Those with a lot of money may have an interest that is different than the community's interests [...] We never understood that he who pays the piper plays the tune. It was a lesson that it doesn't matter whether people love [a team], it's all about the money. I don't think there had been those kinds of things.

> We all know now the sports world is all about making money
> but this was the first time we saw it. This was uprooting a
> club that had all these historical links to the community.

It is striking how closely Gutman's account here echoes the concerns
of Wimbledon's fans at the time of the move: the appreciation of
money overpowering community interests, and the severing of the
historical links. He even reaches for the same horticultural metaphor
as the commission: "uprooting", with its connotations of nurtured
growth over time. And it is easy to see why the idea of franchising
might be anathema to anybody that conceives of a football club as
something constituted by fans in a certain place. It is, in effect, a
total inversion of Robson's definition and a full endorsement of the
principles of Charles Koppel's unique solution: the club inheres in
the ownership, and the place in the league, and all the things that
can be moved; it does not inhere in any of what must be left behind.
Not even the name is safe. Somewhere on their journey inland from
Cascadia, the Seattle Sonics became the Oklahoma City Thunder.

When we look at the motives given and inferred for franchise
moves in American sports, we can see parallels with the move
from Wimbledon to Milton Keynes: a place that cries out for a
sports team, another one that has a team but doesn't deserve it.
The promise of a new stadium, often in the case of the US built
with public funds. More broadly, the promise of making a little or
a lot more money. But the key difference is that professional sports
leagues are closed and established: if Oklahoma City wanted an
NBA team, and the NBA didn't want to expand, then they had to
lure one from elsewhere. There was no Oklahoma City Basketball
waiting to be sugar-daddied up the pyramid. There is no pyramid.

The central importance that the commission placed on avoiding
setting a precedent for franchising in English football is, in effect,
an endorsement of the protesting fan's position that franchising
runs counter to the principles of English football. As noted in
chapter two, the commission sought to evade the question by
presenting a moral case. But perhaps, in a paradoxical way, this
very failure helped them achieve their professed goal. It's not

that franchising hasn't caught on because this wasn't franchising: it plainly and clearly was. Rather, we might conclude that franchising hasn't caught on in part because this exercise was so thoroughly unpleasant that nobody wants to have another crack at it. Indeed, it is *only* the franchising aspect — the purchase of the league place — that has been anything like successful. The name has gone, so too the colours; that never-say-die attitude dissolved when they crossed the Thames. The whole project of Wimbledon-in-MK was quickly abandoned once the team slumped into administration. Røkke and Gjelsten had to write-off millions in unrecoverable debt. And the upward curve to the Premier League never materialised: instead MK Dons have spent most of their time in the middle of League One, with occasional adventures down to League Two and one resoundingly unsuccessful campaign in the Championship. The Asda got built, though. So did the Ikea.

Despite the appeals to morality, no moral precedent was established here: franchising was tried, and found to be unpopular, unpleasant and much harder work than anticipated. Since the move, the idea of rescuing financially struggling teams by moving them somewhere else — however dire their plight, however low their attendances and apparently disengaged their public — has been entirely absent from the conversation. And while the building of new towns has slowed, perhaps limiting the potential for new constituencies of Milton Keynes' size, England certainly hasn't been short of financially struggling teams or imaginative, maverick owners. Dublin is still there, after all, but the football clubs of England seem to be leaving it well alone. Even Winkelman has conceded that his mission hadn't quite gone to plan. "Originally, I thought I could move a football club," he told *Estates Gazette* in 2008. "Now, with hindsight, I've come to realise that you can't." The protesting fans' arguments may not have carried the day, but theirs is the case that has echoed down the years.

* * *

It is at this point that we should take a quick look at what one Tottenham fan described to me as "the tawdry history of the original MK Dons". Until Wimbledon, England's most famous case of a football club actually being moved from one distinct location to another was the relocation of Arsenal in 1913. The club was founded in 1886 as Dial Square by a group of workmen from the Royal Arsenal armaments factory in Woolwich, then part of Kent. They quickly adopted the name of their workplace for their club, and based themselves at the Manor Ground in Plumstead. Royal Arsenal professionalised in 1891 and were invited to join the Football League two years later; they changed their name to Woolwich Arsenal, became the first southern team to join the league, and were promoted from the Second Division to the First in 1904.

Their first visit to the top flight was not a happy one, however, as attendances declined and the club flirted with bankruptcy. Enter the absurdly well-connected Henry Norris: Army colonel, senior Freemason, Conservative MP and future knight of the realm. After an attempt to merge the club with Fulham FC was vetoed by the Football League, he began to look into relocation, and following Arsenal's relegation in 1913, he moved the whole operation across the river Thames to Highbury, some 11 miles away. This called for another name change: they became simply 'The Arsenal'.

There are a number of striking parallels between Norris's grand plan and Winkelman's, nearly a century later. Norris was explicit in his intentions: he was looking for somewhere with a large potential fanbase and excellent transport links; he was leaving behind somewhere out of the way and unglamorous. Nobody appears to have gone as far as arguing that the people of Kent and the south-east edge of London didn't deserve their football team, though it is a neat coincidence that Woolwich Arsenal's fans, like Wimbledon's team, had something of a reputation for rowdiness.

Where the two stories diverge is over the reactions from football's hierarchy and from the fans, considered broadly. There appears to have been some protests from the community that Arsenal were leaving behind; protests that would not have been out of place ninety years later and a few miles west. As Jack Pitt-Brooke has noted in the *Athletic*, the Kentish supporters were "furious", and they even rolled out the f-word:

> Their club was being ripped away from them and there was nothing they could do to stop it. Norris was portrayed by a cartoon in the Woolwich Gazette as kidnapping Kent's only son. 'Mr Norris has decided that financial gain is more important than protecting our local club,' said one letter to the Kentish Gazette. 'He is making a mistake. You cannot 'franchise' a football club. Woolwich Arsenal must stay near Woolwich. People like him have no place in Association football.'

But unlike the case of Wimbledon, this attitude does not appear to have extended to fans beyond those directly implicated. The loudest protests came from the other clubs that would be affected by the move, most notably Arsenal's new north London neighbours Tottenham, who urged the Football League to disallow the move. That effort failed, and then a few years later, when Arsenal won election to the First Division at Spurs' expense, the dynamics and resentments of north London football were fixed for all time.

We can identify several possible reasons for the relative lack of interest from fans beyond Woolwich: the smaller scale of the move; the relative youth of the club; the relative youth of organised football as a whole. The football media landscape was radically different as well, and Arsenal's move does not appear to have occasioned much national attention. And more generally, the sanctity of the footballing pyramid could not possibly have been as much of a concern at the time. For a start, the pyramid was newly under construction, and for an end, it was a thoroughly unsacred space.

Though the pyramid feels both ancient and fundamentally correct, it didn't pop into existence along with the laws of the game in 1863, or even the Football League in 1888, which began as a single division. It was made, and made slowly over time. The Northern League — the second oldest league in the country, founded in 1889 and amateur until 1974 — did not fold into the broader structure until as late as 1991, by which time several of the league's stronger teams had defected to the Northern Premier League. Until they joined the Football League, Arsenal only competed in local cup competitions, under the auspices of the London Football Association, as well as the FA Cup, the only competition theoretically open to any team in the country.

And if the pyramid of the early 20th century amounted to little more than a small pile of rocks, it must also be noted that the rocks were pretty grubby. As mentioned above, Arsenal were not promoted to the First Division in 1919 by sporting means; rather, they were elected at Tottenham's expense, and while allegations of actual bribery have never been substantiated, it seems reasonable to assume that Henry Norris, future Grand Deacon of the United Grand Lodge of England and personal friend of the Archbishop of Canterbury, had no trouble pressing his case. Spurs, at the time, complained of 'irreparable mischief'.

The other team elected to the newly-expanded First Division was Chelsea, who had been relegated on the last day of the 1914/15 season after Manchester United and Liverpool fixed the result of their final game. Seven players were banned, but neither club was sent down. And eight games into the 1919/20 season, Leeds City were dissolved by order of the FA, after refusing to cooperate with an investigation into alleged financial irregularities. If the pyramid was a sacred place, then — compared to match-fixing — crossing the river and heading into town seems a venial sin.

Looking back from 2021, and with allowances for the occasional dedicated Tottenham fan, the idea that Arsenal don't belong in north London is a peculiar one, for the simple reason that they've been there for over a century. Interestingly, a number of my survey respondents predicted that something similar would be necessary for MK Dons to become something like a 'proper' football club. This echoes the ideas of incremental, osmotic change mentioned in chapter six, as well as the idea that it is the repeated process of attending a football club that causes a football club to grow, to take root. Time as both creator and healer.

* * *

Milton Keynes is not the only new town to acquire an old football club. When Telford expanded to incorporate the market town of Wellington, the local side Wellington FC did not move, but changed their name to match their new conurbation. Telford United dissolved in 2004, but were refounded as AFC Telford United that same year. Up in Scotland, in 1994, semi-professional Clyde FC moved from the south east of Glasgow to Cumbernauld, some 15 miles north east. And a year later, in a move bearing a marked similarity to that of Wimbledon, Meadowbank Thistle left Edinburgh and moved 19 miles away to Livingston, where they became Livingston FC.

As with Arsenal decades before, this move appears to have been unpopular with the fans who were losing their club, but failed to outrage the wider footballing public. Meadowbank's attendances before the move were low, often less than a thousand, but more than 4,000 people signed a petition urging the owner, Bill Hunter, to reconsider the move. The battle grew unpleasant: Hunter complained of abuse, while a number of fans found themselves arbitrarily banned from Meadowbank Stadium.

There are a number of important contrasts between Meadowbank in the mid-'90s and Wimbledon in the early noughties, not least Wimbledon's imagination-capturing FA Cup win (Meadowbank had no major honours to their name) and the fact that even in exile at Selhurst Park, Wimbledon's attendances were considerably larger. But perhaps one of the more telling is the difference between the two owners. Røkke and Gjelsten — 'the Norwegians', as they were near-universally known — were clear outsiders, investors from overseas whose only interest in Wimbledon was the possibility of moving it somewhere profitable, initially to Dublin and then to anywhere that would have it. Accordingly Wimbledon's fans were blessed with sympathetic coverage from the local and national press, who — as noted earlier in this chapter — professed horror at the prospect of English football being swept up by the forces of American-flavoured globalisation.

By contrast, Hunter was a local businessman, and even his fan-given nickname, 'Mr Blobby', fails to conjure the same ominous sense of invasion as 'the Norwegians'.[37] And there is also the suggestion that Edinburgh's media, or at least those parts of it that didn't actively support Meadowbank, was simply less interested in defending one of its smaller football clubs. Writing in *WSC* in 1996, a year after Meadowbank moved to Livingston and changed their name, Archie McGregor connects the move to "the seemingly terminal 'also-ran' status of Edinburgh football", and asserts that:

> The demise of the city's third club, Meadowbank Thistle, was precipitated as much by years of shameful indifference by the local press and radio stations as by the draconian manoeuvrings of their reviled chairman, Bill 'Mr Blobby' Hunter. Indeed it's arguable that if Thistle had enjoyed the sort of coverage normally given to a league club within its own town, Blobby would never have attempted, let alone succeeded, in uprooting the club to Livingston. As it is, in an extraordinary challenge to accepted notions about sport being a worthwhile vehicle for the promotion of civic pride and identity, the Edinburgh Evening News actually made Hunter one of its nominees for its 'Local Sports Personality of the Year' award last year. Can you think of any other football city in the UK where someone responsible for closing down one of its clubs would be hailed as some kind of Messianic visionary?

As far as I can tell, Pete Winkelman has never been nominated as Merton's Man of the Year. And it is perhaps indicative that one of the supportive comments from Wimbledon fans in *A Unique Solution to a Unique Problem* states explicitly that the move to Milton Keynes will be "the Livingston answer to the Meadowbank problem". Clearly, in the absence of any sustained media attention, the discontent of Meadowbank's fans hadn't made much of an impression on 'Wimbledon Fan, East Sussex'. Presumably they were more impressed by Livingston FC's return to the Scottish Premier League — three promotions in the six seasons after the move —

---

[37]   Actually, that's not quite right, is it? You know where you are with a horde of marauding Norsemen, but Mr Blobby, who pillaged British living rooms throughout the 1990s, was and remains something far stranger.

and their run, in 2001-02, to the semi-finals of the Scottish Cup. We might assume that had it come about after the Wimbledon saga, such a move would attract greater opprobrium; equally, we might conclude that without widespread national reporting and attention, the ongoing existential issues of many football clubs pass quietly under the radar.

PART 3:
Soul football

Chapter Seven:
Ask a silly question

… And you get, as it turns out, an awful lot of extremely interesting answers. "What is a football club, really, when you get right down to it?" was the final question of my survey and my interviews, tucked away at the end after all the serious, Wimbledon-connected stuff. In a sense, therefore, I was leading my respondents. By positioning this at the end, and not the beginning, it came with the unwritten precondition: *Given all the questions about identity, continuity, and Wimbledon and Milton Keynes we've been discussing, and further to the answers you've already given: what is a football club, really, when you get right down to it?* I suspect the answers I received would have been different, at least in tone, had this question arrived in my respondents' lives entirely without context.

As a question it is perhaps leading in another sense: tacking "really, when you get right down to it" on the end makes this grand, open-ended question sound faintly casual. Flippant, even. Possibly silly.[38] This was me attempting to be clever, not just me keeping myself amused. First, I was attempting to defuse any tension

---

[38] I knew at the time that I was pinching this from a book, though I couldn't remember which one. Looking it up afterwards, I discovered that it is a recurring Terry Pratchett joke, asked in slightly variant forms by a sentient rabbit in *Moving Pictures*, the philosopher Didactylos in *Small Gods* — "Yes, But What's It Really All About, Then, When You Get Right Down To It, I Mean, Really" — and then again by Death in *Soul Music*. Odd what gets stuck in your brain — there must have been more than 20 years between my reading those books and writing the survey.

that might have built up over the rest of the survey: this is still a controversial and living issue, and I was hoping to avoid answers that just read "Who cares? Fuck MK Dons." On this point I was generally but not wholly successful.[39]

Second, I was hoping to make it clear that this question could be answered in similarly light spirits. It is an unusual question, and some of my respondents expressed surprise at being invited to think about it. It is also potentially quite a complicated and even philosophical question, and I wanted to ensure that my respondents were aware that it didn't necessarily require a complicated or philosophical response, and so decide to give no response at all. Thomas Hylland Eriksen has glossed anthropology as "small places, large issues"; adapting that principle, I was looking for small answers to large questions. It seemed to me that this is exactly the kind of large question to which small answers — small in the sense of local and personal, not insignificant — are often the most interesting. Or to put it another way, if your actual answer to the question is "Who cares? Fuck MK Dons", then that's exactly what I was looking for.

There is not space here to reproduce all the responses, as I ended up with more than a thousand in total.[40] The most common answer by quite some distance was "community" or "a community"; many respondents didn't elaborate further. And of course there is no particular need to elaborate further: one can belong to a community without needing or wanting to explain or analyse that belonging. Togetherness is a thing that is lived, not a thing that is written.

But communities of one kind or another form around almost any social activity and, as such, it is interesting to consider what kind of community a football club might be and what character it might have. The most common point of comparison — sometimes as metaphor, sometimes as simile — was 'family'. Familial ideas are commonplace in football discourse, from FIFA's 'football family' —

---

[39]   Heart goes out to whoever responded, simply, "A fucking nightmare."
[40]   If you're interested in seeing the answers, I have set up a Twitter bot @whatisaFC, which will tweet out a few random answers each day. If you'd like the full data set in a more useful way, please contact the publishers.

the favoured administrators, sponsors, and other associated hangers-on who get a huge chunk of the tickets to any World Cup final — to works such as *Family* by Michael Calvin, his account of spending a year embedded with Millwall. From Calvin's introduction:

> Family. It's a concept that covers a multitude of sins, enduring values like loyalty, trust and unconditional love. [...] This book has, as its central subject, a group of working men bound by the challenge of collective achievement. They've allowed me to study the nature of allegiance, the humanity that football is in danger of forfeiting. They represent an endangered species in an age of empty celebrity, a team greater than the sum of its parts. The pressures that assail them, an ordinary yet extraordinary group of sportsmen, will also shape the lives of strangers. Join me in a search for the game's soul ...

A number of my respondents thought along similar lines.

> *A family. A football club is a family full of people who all want one thing. To win and enjoy supporting their club.*

> *A family, a tribe, a feeling of belonging and unconditional loyalty*

> *It is an understanding & a passion of a common interest you share with other people – a family.*

> *A football club is a community and family, it's not about winning or losing, it's about supporting the team throughout.*

Yet there is something distinctly un-familial about what happened to Wimbledon, something that threatens the very nature of the comparison. Families of any type are often fractious and divided, occasionally beyond all hope of reconciliation. Yet familial bonds at their most fundamental are always present and fundamentally indissoluble: even disowning a relative does not stop them being just that. The strength of the family metaphor depends on the parallel between a family and this football-adjacent entity, created through repeated association and positive mutual identification. How do we fit Wimbledon, and the split, into this? The idea of MK

Dons as something cast out and disowned doesn't quite ring true, as such ideas contain within them the possibility, however remote, of reconciliation. What is cast out can be welcomed back; what is disowned can be reclaimed. The prodigal son can always come home. The tenor of comment on MK Dons, however, suggests a split not just of conduct but of category. As one respondent put it, MK Dons are "a football club that should not exist". Or another: "MK Dons aren't a football club, they're an abomination".[41]

There is a more general point here too. If football clubs are families and if two thirds of fans feel that the operational part of that club — their family — doesn't care about their interests, then the familial model of a football club is deeply dysfunctional. Either this idea of a family specifically excludes the owners and administrators in a lot of cases or, against received wisdom, all these families are unhappy in the same way. Family might be the most common point of comparison, but the prevalence and nature of this particular kind of discontent suggest that this is as much aspiration as description.

---

[41]   The idea of MK Dons as an "abomination" is a suggestive one: not necessarily in the censorious sense — this is abominable! take it away! — but in the Lovecraftian sense of a thing that should not be. In 2012, ahead of the first meeting of AFC Wimbledon and MK Dons, Robbie Savage asked in the Mirror: "I don't want to be obtuse about this, but why is MK Dons' FA Cup tie with AFC Wimbledon a grudge match?" If he wasn't being obtuse then he was being provocative, and he went on to say that had the club not moved to Milton Keynes "they would have gone out of existence altogether". But he had the germ of a point, in that a grudge match is something ordinary: what Manchester United used to have with Arsenal; what England think they have with Germany. The term is wholly inadequate for AFC vs. MK Dons; so too 'derby', 'rivalry', and all the other labels football has for games between teams that don't get on for one reason or another. Like a weird fiction protagonist struggling with geometry that defies sense, colours that ordinary eyes cannot perceive, and all the other indescribable features of something so alarmingly other that it evades — perhaps even destroys — description, ordinary football discourse simply does not have the language or the concepts to accurately describe ... well, I've written myself into a corner here. Whatever it is that is going on when a franchise fights a phoenix.

Though not deployed quite as frequently as 'family', another suggestive and recurrent description offered by my respondents was, in line with Rob Brady's sentiments at the end of chapter five, the idea of a soul, or a spirit, or some other intangible *thing* that plays a crucial role in defining a football club.[42] There were many variations on this theme, both in answering this question and the earlier question regarding continuity between Wimbledon and either MK Dons or AFC Wimbledon. Some respondents characterised the club itself as being the soul of its local area.

> *The heart and soul of a local community (sounds a bit poncey but you know what I mean).*

Some invoked the soul in a negative sense, distinct in its absence from Milton Keynes, from MK Dons, and from MK Dons' ground Stadium MK.

> *MK is a disgrace. The stadium is soulless and it has set an awful precedent that clubs in future will surely look to take advantage of.*

> *Fuck Milton Keynes it's an awful place that's soulless and the football club represents that entirely in my opinion.*

> *AFC Wimbledon has the soul of Wimbledon FC. MK Dons doesn't have one.*

That last quote is particularly interesting as it suggests that this thing — this soul, this spirit — is something that was present in Wimbledon and has somehow been transferred to AFC Wimbledon. This idea recurred again and again, particularly in the context of my questions around continuity: that a club has a spirit or a soul of some kind, and that this had passed from Wimbledon to AFC Wimbledon, and not to MK Dons.

---

[42] I should probably clarify here that the spirit of a football club is distinct from 'the spirit of the game' in a sporting sense, which concerns the unwritten moral rules that bind footballers, such as 'kicking the ball out for an injury' and 'kicking the ball back to the team that kicked the ball out for an injury'. This sort of thing is much more important in cricket, anyway. We can safely ignore it.

> *Fans carry the 'spirit' of the club: they 'own' what it represents, whether owners have the deeds or not.*
>
> *AFC Wimbledon are the spiritual continuation of Wimbledon FC*
>
> *they are Wimbledon reincarnated*
>
> *[a football club] is situated in a physical location but its essence is ethereal*
>
> *The body became mk dons and the soul is in afc*

What kind of thing might this soul, this spirit, be? I do not propose to spend any time unpicking the various parallels and differences with any particular religion's ideas about the soul, for the simple reason that none of my respondents identified a particular religion: this soul is a generic soul. And importantly there seems to be no relationship between whatever this soul is and a God, or gods, which seems an obvious sticking point. More modern thinking on the idea of a soul might not be any more useful: one of my interviewees laughed at and dismissed the idea of a football club having "a Schopenhauerian will". But if you mention the idea of something non-human possessing a soul to an anthropology professor, as I did shortly after collating my responses, they will shout with delight. "Animism! Animism!"

Attempting a comprehensive definition of animism in all its varieties is almost certainly futile, but an evocative formulation comes from anthropologist Graham Harvey: "The world is full of persons, only some of whom are human." Very, very crudely put, it is a collective term for any of the hundreds if not thousands of belief systems that hold that souls or spiritual essences of some kind exist not just in humans, but in animals, places, and other entities; sometimes this is taken to confer a kind of personhood or some other form of spiritual character beyond that which an animal, place, or other entity might typically, by a non-animist, be assumed to possess.

Western anthropologists have been bundling all these disparate beliefs together under the label of "animism" almost since the emergence of the discipline itself, and indeed we should address these early accounts first. It would be simple, straightforward, and in my view entirely incorrect to take, say, Edward Tylor's "developing doctrine of spiritual beings", first published in 1871, in which he noted that some "primitives" have —

> An idea of pervading life and will in nature [...], a belief in personal souls animating even what we call inanimate bodies, a theory of transmigration of souls as well in life after death.

— and transfer this structure wholesale onto football fans, asserting some kind of parallel like: the fan is to their club as the 'primitive' is to their totem. To do so would be to do a great disservice to all parties, and not just because we have, hopefully, moved beyond the Victorian hierarchies of the primitive and the civilised. We know that football club owners often view their fans as a lumpen inferior mass; we do not have to accept this framing.

To return to the soul of a football club, then. As far as I can tell from my responses, none of the fans that suggested that a football club has a soul were suggesting, by implication, that the club was a person of any kind. But if not theological or personalising this soul is, at the very least, animating. David Hume wrote that humanity possesses a fundamental tendency towards prosopopoeia, a quite tremendous word that I urge you to say out loud right now. "We find human faces in the moon," he wrote, "armies in the clouds". And though the face in the moon begins as a coincidence of shape, it nevertheless imparts to the moon a character, a sense of life. The moon watches, the clouds march. So what, then, does the soul of a football club do; or, perhaps more precisely, what do football clubs do that causes people to look at them and see a soul? Turns out, all sorts of things.

Chapter Eight:
A metaphysical John O'Shea

As I collated and considered the responses to my survey, and began to pick out those that mentioned some kind of soul, spirit, or other intangible *thing* — I'll use 'soul; as the catch-all from hereon — it quickly became clear that not everybody conceived of this soul in the same way, or imagined this soul doing the same thing. For some it was a way of labelling or imagining the thing that fans make when they come together, repeatedly, to watch the same football team play game after game. Some imagined the soul as inherent to or emplaced within a particular and significant location, often the football ground; the corollary to this is the idea of a soul as something notable by its absence from a given place or stadium, a perceived soullessness not limited to Milton Keynes and MK Dons. Some invoked the idea to explain just how continuity was maintained from Wimbledon FC to AFC Wimbledon: a thing that was present within one club and then transferred or decanted along to the next. And a few shifted the metaphor altogether, positioning the club itself as the soul within the broader community.

When it comes to a football club, then, the soul is a utility player. A flexible all-rounder that can do almost anything it is asked to; that can slot into a number of positions within a wider conception of the form and function of football clubs.

A thing that is made together

[A club is] a combination of history, location, a group of people and a collective identity.

When it comes to football clubs, the idea of the productive collective is a resonant and recurrent one. I have already noted the popularity of 'community' as a catch-all definition for a club, and as discussed in part one, Kennedy's account of the formation of football clubs hinges on this identity emerging from a group enjoying their mutual interest together, which is then sold back to them as the football club. This manifests at a particular, individual level as well: to go to a football club is to experience a collective from within. To pick one example from many, here is journalist Iain Macintosh describing his first visit to Roots Hall.

> The football was, for numerous reasons, secondary to the terraces. It was a sideshow. This was a throbbing, sweating, burping, farting and cussing collective of mind and heart.

Even the language of football is suggestive: an *audience* can be any size, but football has *crowds*, and here the noun brings the verb along with it. Crowds are close, even claustrophobic; they have size beyond easy comprehension, particularly from within.

Perhaps the most celebrated depiction of a football crowd coming into being, of the individuals cohering into one great mass, is L.S. Lowry's 1953 painting *Going to the Match*. On the left of the picture is a stark chunk of Bolton Wanderers' old ground Burnden Park, lost to the wrecking balls in 1997; on the right, the end of a row of terraced houses, with another terrace shadowed behind. Beyond the housing, hazy in the distance, sit the chimneys and silos of industrial Lancashire. And around this all, flowing from the houses and factories into the narrow doors of the stadium, a great tide of people, rushing from the splintered loneliness of the working world to the togetherness of Saturday afternoon, 3 o'clock.

Lowry's figures are famously featureless: they have faces by implication and presumption, the occasional hint of moustache notwithstanding. But look at *Going to the Match* long enough and you start to realise that the lack of particular features does not lead to a lack of particularity. The matchstick people may not have faces but they are distinguished from one another by clothing and physique: mostly blacks and greys and browns, but with occasional moments of brightness here and there. One figure, crossing the road in the foreground, matches a red hat and coat; to their left is an even brighter hat, paired with a more muted overcoat. There are shades of orange and blue; there are stout figures walking beside thin ones. At the very bottom right of the picture, one figure in ochre with a red bundle on their back — a parent and a baby, perhaps — seems to be looking directly out of the canvas, through the fourth wall, back at the viewer. These are individuals, even as they pass into and become part of the crowd; indeed, the nature of the crowd is imparted not through each fan coming to resemble every other, but through the assertion of mutual connectedness between individuals.

We might even go further and suggesting that joining a football crowd can be reindividuating. The crowd can act as a shelter, as a space in which an individual is cloaked, camouflaged, and free from scrutiny, and so better able to express themselves. This does not hold for everyone, of course: football crowds are kinder places than they once were, but they can still be unpleasant and hostile. But in theory, everybody is here for the same reason; everybody is on the same side. And within this protective canopy of mutual interest, one can find oneself by losing oneself.

We can perhaps demonstrate this by a negative. There is a unique terror to self-expression within a noisy crowd, and that is the moment in which you shout something just as everybody else falls silent. Your witticism — not so witty now — echoes around. At that moment you are by your own hubris ejected from the collective. Everybody is looking at you, and there is one single moment of perfect and terrible isolation, before the laughter — some good-natured, some probably not — rushes up and swallows you back into the whole.

In any case, at the risk of seeming a terrible Lowry hipster, there is another, earlier painting that even better illustrates the process of forming a club, of creating this collective. *The Football Match* was painted in 1949 and shares most of the same component parts as *Going to the Match*, but here all are reconfigured to more ominous, less kinetically rousing effect. We are zoomed much further out: the terraced houses sit squat and dark in the foreground, while the industrial tangle of chimneys and warehouses begins halfway up the canvas with a slash of stark red and black, before filling most of the top half of the frame. And in between the two is the titular football match and, significantly, a complete lack of a football ground. Instead, the matchstick people — here tiny and truly deindividuated — are all still. They do not flow, they stand and watch. The markings on the pitch are impossibly faint; the goal frames are there, just about, almost by implication. The few players we can see are tiny dots.

What makes this a football match, then, and not just a mass of people, is the fact that the fans have organised themselves as spectators around a football pitch, delineating the space of the game and so the game itself. A hollowed oblong of engaged and interested humanity, watching the game and asserting, in the process, that football is *the thing the crowd stands around*. It is a literal instantiation of Jock Stein's maxim, these days seen on banners at every level of the game in its remixed form: football without fans is nothing. Indeed, one could almost cast *The Football Match* as a conceptual prequel to *Going to the Match*: this is the early stage of the repeated, interested attendance that leads, over time, to the emergence of football clubs — these clubs will later build football grounds over the shapes already defined by the fans.

> *A social construct that is embodied in the spirit and soul of the supporters.*

> *It is the abstract — the spirit, the beacon of light for fans, that collective passion and link to the community in terms of supporting the team where you grew up/live - that is the most important aspect.*

Football fans are generally aware of their importance, en masse, in the creation of football as it is experienced by both themselves and the wider interested public, even and perhaps especially where they chafe against the market logics that define and control their experience.

Football without fans is still a game, after all; the players enjoy it on their own terms. But a football club without fans is just an empty building with a game in it. A piece of land, behind a house, with hardly anybody there; a far less interesting painting.

Perhaps the soul, in this deployment, refers to something like: the identity that was first created, then sustained, by the repeated gathering of a football crowd aware of itself as a football crowd, as a community constructing itself over time. 'Soul' points to and evokes the character of the thing that was commodified as the club was created and has been continually sold back to the fans ever since. I should acknowledge here that I suspect most football fans would not use the term 'soul'; however, I suggest that many will acknowledge that there is a thing, of some kind or another, identifiable if not quite definable, that is created by this repeated interest and gathering through time. A shared intangible that emerges from the communality in which they and others are absorbed. More on this in chapter ten.

Circuit makers

> [A club is] the sporting representation of a place or community.

To return once again to Bobby Robson, consider the positive part of his definition: "It's the noise, the passion, the feeling of belonging, the *pride in your city*" (my emphasis). Or consider the importance of place to Lowry's paintings of football fans. Here's Scott Oliver in the *Blizzard*, on *Going to the Match*: the club in the picture "is rooted in the surrounding locale, an autochthonous expression of the community. It is territorialised: a stable, regularised circuit of 'individual' behaviours, social relations and libidinal investments providing what Raymond Williams called a 'structure of feeling'." We'll come back to the idea of a structure of feeling in chapter ten, but for now, that image of a "stable, regularised circuit" is a sharp one: this is an ongoing process, repeated motion through defined patterns giving rise to a kind of energy.

Many if not most football fans have matchday patterns, whether they be simple habits or self-conscious rituals. Often there is little spectacular about them: to get to Champion Hill from our old house in Peckham, my wife and I would walk the same route each Saturday afternoon or Tuesday night, the same path from one home to another. And along the way a coffee from the little van in Peckham Square, a pint in the EDT, a chance to say hello, hey, afternoon, evening, alright. A flare of superstition: don't tie your scarf to your belt until you're in the pub, Andrew; don't you dare wait until afterwards. Usual place near the dugouts, or usual place behind the goal. Always the same each week, always not quite the same; characterful variations within character-defining habits.

Taken on an individual basis this is just one not particularly exciting story of going to the match, but any given game sees hundreds if not thousands of these stories all coming together in the same place. Further up the pyramid, tens of thousands. Taken all together, these are the particulars of the process of supporting that club. And so moving a club is not just a question of weighing up the profit margins and promising to keep the shirt. It is a circuit breaker: an act of terminal violence to each and every one of these patterns. As far as Wimbledon are concerned, it is significant that even before the split, the club was effectively running a long-term experiment into the consequences of relocation as it applies to football clubs. Selhurst Park was not so far that the club altogether lost any connection with Merton, and the move was never asserted as permanent, but there seems to be little doubt that essentially everybody hated it. The club couldn't keep as much of the matchday revenue as they might in their own ground, and many fans had to make an awkward journey to a ground they didn't enjoy visiting. According to one fan: "Ask any Dons supporter and they would be able to count on their fingers of one hand the enjoyable experiences at Selhurst Park." Or as David Conn put it: "the club's soul was freezing over at Selhurst". There were practical consequences too, as *Mirror* journalist Tony Stenson recalled:

Selhurst Park was a disastrous move for Wimbledon. I remember walking down Wimbledon High Street over the years. In the early days all you would see were Liverpool shirts everywhere, but by 1991 mothers had started buying Wimbledon shirts instead. There was a whole generation coming through — you could see it. The club had the chance to grow and they blew it.

To be a guest is to be in somebody else's space, however pleasant the place and however gracious and understanding your hosts. While in dispute with the property developers that owned Champion Hill, Dulwich Hamlet played the end of the 2017/18 season and the beginning of the next at the home of their local rivals Tooting & Mitcham United. This was a longer journey for plenty of fans, including myself, but not for everybody. Yet even those who lived closer and so were now in theory better able to attend were keen that this arrangement be over as soon as possible. It was somebody's home; it wasn't ours. And as a place already occupied, it wasn't a place that we could start to make ours. It is poignant to look back at the footage of the last game of the season, in which Dulwich finally sealed promotion to the Conference South after several seasons of collapsing in the playoffs, and watch the Dulwich fans — me, friends, and family somewhere among them — celebrate the winning penalty by spilling onto the wrong pitch.[43]

There is another peculiar wrinkle to the Wimbledon saga that illustrates the importance of place. Initially, along with the league position, MK Dons took the patrimony of the forerunning club: the trophies and memorabilia, including a replica of the 1988 FA Cup. This was of course controversial, and in 2004, as part of a deal brokered by the Football Supporters' Federation, they handed the

---

[43] I'm going to hide this bit down in the footnotes but, while Imperial Fields certainly wasn't home, it was and remains a pretty decent stadium. Some might even say a better one than Champion Hill. I'm a particular fan of the two end terraces with huge coverings — by non-league standards — that wouldn't look out of place in Christopher Herwig's photobook of modernist Soviet bus stops.

patrimony back — but not to AFC Wimbledon. Instead they passed them to the London borough of Merton, where Wimbledon's old Plough Lane had been located and where AFC's new Plough Lane ground has been built. They were given to the location, to be reclaimed upon returning home.

The importance of place to a football club, and to that part of a football club's identity that is made by the fans, is not just a question of the name on the badge or the convenience of the journey. It matters that this particular thing has been made in this particular place, since the very nature of the place has influenced, shaped, and informed the nature of the thing: the people, the geography, the history; the streets, the smells, the angle of the sunshine over the main stand; the multivariant threads of the social and cultural fabric in which the club and all its fans are enmeshed. As noted in chapter two, it is not just that clubs come from places: they are *of* places, brought out of them and tied into them by this circuit of human behaviours.

Thinking more generally about the soul of a club, we can easily see how a soul connected to a place, and created over time, might be absent from a club that has just been moved elsewhere, whether 60 miles north or 1,500 miles south-east. American journalist Bill Simmons has referred to the Oklahoma City Thunder as the "zombie Sonics", a thing physically alive but soulless and socially dead. And as already seen, with regard to MK Dons, a number of my survey respondents made comments along the following lines:

> *While the components of the club's identity may evolve over time, it needs to be a gradual process that still remains within the community area.*

As suggested in chapters five and six, if Milton Keynes and MK Dons amount to a disquieting irruption to the normal slow processes of forming, respectively, a town and a football club, then it is only by allowing these slow processes to reassert themselves over time that something approaching propriety might be achieved. It remains to be seen if time is sufficient to change popular perceptions of MK Dons, but it will certainly be necessary if they are to establish themselves as a club of their new place, as a focus for all these personal patterns.

Empty seats and echoing stands

There are souls, and then there not-souls: the spaces where a soul might be. When it comes to MK Dons, this is an accusation levelled variously at the club —

> *MK Dons are a soulless plastic club which should have no place in the English league.*

— and at the place itself —

> *That kind of thing can't be transferred to another place especially one as soulless as MK.*

— and also, frequently, at their ground, Stadium MK.

> *I've been to Stadium MK. It just doesn't feel like football. It's located in a retail park and feels much more like it was built to be monetised through concerts and that sort of thing. It all felt very American.*

Of course, the Dons are far from the only club so burdened. Some quick Googling suggests plenty of allegedly soulless grounds around the world, including some of the most famous: Arsenal's Emirates stadium; the new Wembley; Juventus' former ground the Stadio delle Alpi; Barcelona's Camp Nou; and, most notoriously in recent years, West Ham's new home, the converted London Olympic Stadium. When it comes to grounds, the sense of soullessness is often intimately related to the question of atmosphere. Reflecting in 2020 on Arsenal's move to the Emirates, Arsène Wenger explicitly invoked the idea of a soul as a thing that was left behind after the move, and tied that to the architecture of the stadium and its impact on the atmosphere.

> I moved from Highbury, which was similar to Anfield, but there was a soul in the stadium. We built a new stadium but we never found our soul — we left our soul at Highbury.

We could never recreate it for security reasons. The distance from the pitch to the stand had to be bigger as we needed ambulances to come in. The inclination of the stands had to be smaller, all those things together that we didn't find to recreate the atmosphere.

The soul, then, is awakened by — or perhaps glimpsed thanks to — the atmosphere. And atmosphere itself is a similarly slippery concept, often taken to simply mean 'loud' but in truth something more complex. An ideal atmosphere is welcoming to some and hostile to others, encouraging to your team and your fans while simultaneously intimidating to theirs. An atmosphere is altered by myriad factors: how full a ground is, who it is full with, how a ground is designed, how the respective teams are playing, how the home crowd feel about their team or their owners, the weather, the significance of the game, and so on. There is also the question of location: many of the more hated modern grounds are located out of town, outside the usual fabric of the city. They are places to which fans have to commute, surely the most soulless form of travel, one that interrupts the Lowry-like flow from home to ground and alters the experience for the worse. This has been a particular source of concern for West Ham fans, attending games out in the Olympic Park, a vast and windy monument to the forces of gentrification snuggled up against Westfield Stratford shopping centre. An *Observer* report in 2018 quoted several fans lamenting their former ground at Upton Park.

This place is soulless ... It's got nothing. I used to go to Upton Park, grab a programme, nip in the pie and mash, have a bet, into the boozer, meet my pals, all good, have a laugh, then out afterwards. I've got nish here. I'm out in the elements drinking beer out of a plastic glass.

I don't smell any burgers and onions.

You go down to Upton Park and there's boozers right by the ground. It was all locals and the market, and you had the Asian community. There was Nathan's, the pie and eel shop, people used to queue up round the corner. It was just part of the match-day experience.

Within football grounds, individual factors also alter the atmosphere as it is experienced by any given fan, including where they are standing or sitting and who they are standing or sitting with. Non-league games, rarely full and often played in grounds with little to no capacity to retain noise, can seem almost entirely without atmosphere as such, yet as a fan a non-league game can feel, in certain circumstances, significantly more intense than some far bigger games with allocated and controlled seating. I have been to knock-out Champions League games at Old Trafford, as part of a crowd of around 60,000, and Isthmian League games with Dulwich in crowds that number in the hundreds, and the latter have at times felt significantly more *atmospheric*, whether it be on a good day as part of a small, tightly-knit, joyous group, singing and clapping and drinking on my own terms, or all wrapped up in the taut nervous energy of another play-off defeat. Although it's probably safe to assume that this communicates itself less to the players, out of hearing at the other end of the pitch, than the noise of tens of thousands, even if they are just shuffling their feet.

As well as the dispiriting architecture, the sense of declining atmosphere at some English grounds has been blamed in part on the removal of standing terraces in the top two tiers, following the recommendations of the Taylor Report. Some English fans look with envy at the large terraces of German football, and a few clubs have begun to take tentative steps towards reintroducing standing sections with rail seating or other safe standing architecture. Some have also looked into designated 'singing sections', in the hope that the noisier fans can amplify their efforts through proximity, then inspire other sections of the ground to join in. The price of top-tier football has also come under fire: following a Premier League football team is an expensive business and England is a country of significant inequality and, in recent years, biting austerity. Premier League crowds have been growing steadily older and wealthier over time, and numbers are bolstered with tourists. They also seem to have been growing quieter: even proverbially atmospheric Anfield can be prone to long stretches of silence in the absence of anything immediately exciting.

Perhaps we might define atmosphere as the crowd asserting itself within the context of the match: responding to events on the field but also feeding back into them. An ongoing, chaotic, at times overwhelming commentary, not merely descriptive but responsive and even recursive, expressed at times in words, at times in song, occasionally with booing, and at times through a kind of extra-linguistic howl. It can be encouraging or discouraging, condemnatory or celebratory; it can express and inspire joy or giddiness or quivering nervousness both in the crowd itself and in the players. This is all mediated by the architecture and the context in which support is performed: the steepness or otherwise of the stands, any roof that keeps the noise in, the iron fist of the stewarding. If Wenger is right, then perhaps the soul of a football club in this context is what can be apprehended — can be *felt* — when a maximally inclusive crowd is given the platform and the licence to *be a crowd* to the fullness of its capacity and desire.

Decantability

It seems clear that Wimbledon FC and AFC Wimbledon are not two separate clubs in the sense that, say, Carmarthen Town and Boca Juniors are separate clubs: wholly unconnected entities that share virtually nothing beyond the basic fact that both are football clubs. As noted earlier, when registering as a club with the FA, AFC Wimbledon listed their year of foundation as 1889 rather than 2001, and the FA registered them as such. But it was interesting to note, however, that just over half of my survey respondents felt that AFC Wimbledon could not be said to be the winners of the 1988 FA Cup, suggesting that a certain kind of separation is perceived by some. Yet my survey respondents also felt, by a thumping majority, that AFC are the continuation of Wimbledon.

MK Dons are the business continuation, AFC are the continuation of the soul of the club.

This question has been put directly to one of the move's major protagonists. Once the club was established in Milton Keynes, and the name change to MK Dons had been confirmed, Pete Winkelman was asked about the 'true spirit' of Wimbledon FC, and whether it was now being carried by AFC Wimbledon. He rejected the idea —

> Good God, no. I think that both the MK Dons and AFC Wimbledon share the same heritage, but we're the real child of Wimbledon, because of the actions of the AFC Wimbledon Group: they left their team before their team left them.

— but he did not reject the framing, instead choosing to present MK Dons as the continuation. It appears custody of the soul was important to both sides of the argument.[44]

Most of the responses to my survey were sympathetic to AFC Wimbledon in a broad sense, even those that were largely unmoved by the wider issues of club identity and franchising. But there were two notable themes that might broadly be considered 'anti-AFC'. The first centres around Kingsmeadow, AFC's home from 2003, which had previously belonged to Kingstonian; the former owners stayed on as tenants until 2017, when AFC sold the ground to Chelsea, who now use it as the home ground of their women's team and a base for their academy.[45] Kingstonian are now based 10 miles away, ground-sharing with Leatherhead. According to a *Guardian* piece from Kingstonian's final game at Kingsmeadow, the feeling among Kingstonian fans was varied and nuanced, ranging from the belief that "Wimbledon's generosity has in fact sustained Kingstonian for well over a decade" — AFC charged Kingstonian low rent as tenants, and passed on £1m of the proceeds of the

---

[44] His preferred metaphor of parent to 'child' suggests the existence of Wimbledon DNA, to go alongside the more glamorous and widely known Arsenal DNA and Barcelona DNA. It does also give the whole business the air of a sharp-elbowed parent buying their way into a well-heeled catchment area.

[45] Kingsmeadow, at least when I was last there watching Dulwich, is a gorgeous little ground, close and intimate and wonky in all the ways that make watching non-league football precious.

sale — to the sense that "Wimbledon have turned away from the values that used to set them apart". Throughout that last game, a rash of stickers appeared around the ground comparing AFC with MK Dons. Though as far as I can tell, a strong view on the rights or wrongs of this situation doesn't make any difference to any perceived connection between WFC and AFC: any perceived sins of the new club doesn't seem to render them unconnected to the old.

The other line of criticism — which, as far as I could tell, tended to come from MK Dons fans rather than disgruntled non-league fans — is that outlined by Winkelman above: that the fans left their club before their club left them. This, as far as criticisms go, has the strength of being technically correct. AFC Wimbledon's first league campaign was the 2002/03 season; that same campaign, Wimbledon FC played out one last uninspiring season at Selhurst Park. As a criticism it has also been advanced by a few of Wimbledon's players at the time. Malvin Kamara, who came through the youth teams and made two appearances for Wimbledon in their last full season at Selhurst Park, then 86 over the next three seasons for Wimbledon and MK Dons, told the MK Dons podcast *Sit Down or We'll Steal Your Club*[46] that the contrast between Selhurst Park's empty stands — "a ghost town" — and the booming crowds at AFC Wimbledon rankled with the players.

> When AFC Wimbledon was set up, they were getting full grounds. I was like 'Hold on a minute, where were you when we were going through the hard times and Selhurst Park was almost empty?' You can't then turn around and say 'How dare you take the club away from us' — when the club got relegated, you disappeared. I remember at the time talking to the players and thinking the cheek of it to be upset with the club, but when the club needed you the most, when we got relegated from the Premier League, you turned your back on it and no longer wanted to turn up at Selhurst Park. They were all turning up to AFC games but not in the Championship because we were no longer playing against

---

[46] Which I think we can all agree is the only possible name for an MK Dons podcast.

> Manchester United ... I don't know how they can form AFC,
> jump on it because it was a bit of a fad and watch them in
> non-league. Their attendance was higher in non-league than
> it was in the Championship.[47]

You can understand how, for the players, the sight of an empty
stadium and the reports of partying elsewhere might feel like
abandonment. And Kamara is certainly right to suggest that the
fans could have done otherwise. They could have stayed to watch
Wimbledon play out their last campaign in south London, and
only started the process of founding a new club once the move had
actually happened and the club were playing in Milton Keynes.
Certainly this would have shielded the fans from the charge of
quitting before they were quitted. But this suggestion — that the
crowd should continue to turn up regardless of circumstances until
it becomes literally impossible — rather rests on that reductive,
prescriptive model of football support we've already encountered.
Indeed, a reductive, prescriptive model of human nature. For years,
Wimbledon fans had been asked to go to somebody else's ground
to watch an increasingly poor team play increasingly poor football
while the owners agitated behind the scenes. Now they were being
asked to do that in the certain knowledge that the team would be
leaving at the end of the season. Set that against the possibility of
building something new, something exciting, something yours ...
of doing it again and doing it right. This might be hindsight, but
it barely feels like a choice at all. The idea that football fans owe
unthinking, unflinching fealty to their club, whatever indignities or
inconveniences it inflicts upon them, here failed to survive contact
with the idea of the club actually moving away.

The other option would be for the fans to stay and fight some
more, to not just see the season out but to protest through it —

---

[47] It appears that Kamara doesn't quite have his timings right here.
Wimbledon were relegated from the Premier League in May 2000, but the
announcement of the move didn't come until the following summer, and
the foundation of AFC the summer after that. Wimbledon's attendances
at Selhurst Park were never great, but the 'almost empty' stage came after
two Manchester United-less campaigns in the second tier.

this has, of course, a certain romantic appeal. But this was a fanbase that had seen a decision from the FA that would have kept the club in place overturned by an opaque commission on the basis that they, the fans, didn't care about the club enough. Think again of "I just want to watch football." Even now, many years and a lot of watched football later, you can hear the fatigue rolling off those words. We can never know whether another round of protests might have had some effect; if there was one weird trick that would have kept the club where it was. But it seems understandable that Wimbledon's fans got tired of looking. In the end, the founders of AFC took the moment of the move's confirmation as the event horizon.

But the overlap does raise an interesting question as to the identity of the clubs. It is not simply that the club ceased to exist in Wimbledon, then cohered again just down the road, all in neat and tidy chronological order. Instead the fans formed a new club while the old was still hanging around, and years down the line a motley collection of football fans scraped from the internet agreed by a large majority that this new club possessed a continuity with the club that they left behind.

> *The difference of the legal continuation against the spiritual soul of the club.*

> *afc are a completely new club, they have the clearer dotted line history, but it's. Not a simple continuation. The body became mk dons and the soul is in afc. But neither are Wimbledon.*

I do not mean to suggest that Stewart and the rest of AFC's founders and fans carried 'the soul' knowingly and grandly before them, encased in a golden ark to inspire the wandering tribes of Wimbledon. (Although, as quoted at the end of chapter five, Rob Brady suggests just this kind of salvage-reification in *An Undividable Glow*: "Part of us has gathered what we believe to be the soul and wrapped it in the softest of cotton and placed it gently into a treasure chest for its protection ..."). Instead, they laid claim to the name and the history and they transferred the practice: the regular, repeated, interested processes of following and watching a football club. And as this was much the same people in much the same place, professing to be supporting their club this season just as they had supported their club last, so a continuity of identity became apparent to those not immediately involved. If it is this process that gives rise to the thing that we might call the soul, then the continuation of this process through what is technically another club serves to demonstrate where this soul emerges from and by whom it is maintained.

The club is the soul

[A football club] should be the heart and soul of a city/town — something for locals to bond over.

One interesting deployment of the idea of a soul is to place it not within the football club, but instead to designate the club as the soul of its local community. This chimes with the account of my interviewee Charlie, who drew an analogy with a parish church, and cast the fans as the congregation:

The role of the church is sort of for it to stay there and be the constant and if people want to waver in their level of belief and then come back, that's up to them.

Here the club is identified as performing a function within the wider social structure of a community. Deploying the idea of a soul in this way serves to emphasise the fundamental integration of a club with its locale, while simultaneously positioning the club itself as a public good: a place of celebration, congregation and spiritual nourishment. There is also a certain amount of functional overlap as well: club bars can be turned to many of the same ends as church halls or community halls. At a higher level, the meeting rooms of larger stadiums are used to host conferences, exams, and networking events. Clubs can act as the locus around which a community socialises and organises, and almost every club in England has some manner of community engagement programme, from relationships with local schools to food bank collections. Of course, this idea of a club as something that enriches a local area is contested: football is not socially all-consuming, and both apathy and antipathy can be found around almost every club. But it's interesting that even the Stadium MK consortium had to advance some version of this theory: the public good, set against the furniture store and the supermarket. Of course, at the same time, Koppel was telling the residents of Merton that football fans make for terrible neighbours, so a certain amount of cynicism seems appropriate.

And were such a club to be moved, then the soul of the area would be gone as well. Here, to briefly hop back across the Atlantic, is the beginning of a *Los Angeles Times* review of a biography of Walter O'Malley, the man who moved the Dodgers across the United States: "To Brooklynites of a certain age, Dodgers owner Walter O'Malley was a money-grubbing weasel who ripped the soul from their community when he announced he was moving to L.A."

This idea of a club-as-soul suggests not one but two problems for any moving club: not just the space it would leave behind, but how well regarded it might be once it arrives. According to one MK Dons fan I spoke to, the arrival of the Dons created "a buzz" around the town and attendances were "not bad" for bigger matches, but "what it lacked and still does were die-hard fans. The ones that would sing and go and see them in all weathers … Cold weather and crap opponents and the attendances would be far lower." He also suggests that for many MK residents, the Dons amount to their second team, which certainly suggests that the club haven't yet acquired the status of 'soul of the community'. However, many of my respondents stressed that MK Dons community work, particularly their connections with local schools, is highly thought of in Milton Keynes; as previously noted, this may just be a question of time that must be served.

Chapter Nine:
'Against Modern Football'

There is one more deployment of the word 'soul' which is worth our attention. Indeed, along with the idea of a soulless stadium, it is perhaps the most common context in which the word 'soul' appears in football conversation. It applies not to any specific football club nor to the sport as it is played on the pitch, but to the game generally and broadly: The Soul of Football. The most notable thing about the soul of football is that, as with these half-empty and quiet grounds, it is generally discovered in its absence, whether actual or imminent. Sometimes it is critically endangered; other times it hasn't been seen for years and is feared lost, trampled underfoot as the game marches forward. Look back through the last few decades and you can find a thread of argument dedicated to finding, saving, and preserving this soul, if possible. And if not, then to marking and lamenting its departure.

There was, as might be expected, a lot of this about in April 2021, during the brief and spectacular flaming of the Super League across the sporting horizon. I'll come back to the Super League in general later on, but one of the more common objections focused on the proposed format, a closed system largely apart from the European football pyramids in which 15 teams would be guaranteed a place no matter their performance in the previous season. It would also have the effect of violently uprooting the Super League clubs from their contexts, relegating the competitions that made them to a secondary concern. As one banner outside Arsenal's stadium put it:

You stole our crest, we stayed
You took our home, we moved
Wherever you went, we followed
Whatever price you demanded, we paid
All for you to go & sell our soul!

A cynic would suggest that the acquiescence of the first four lines might have encouraged the owners into believing that this move might fly; a cynic might have a point. Nevertheless it seems clear that the idea of England's clubs placing a closed continental competition well above their domestic campaign was a step too far for many fans, even those that generally saw no problem with their club's economically-reinforced position above the rest.

But the prospect of the Super League, however brief, wasn't the beginning of the search for football's soul. In August 2019, in the *Independent*, journalist Miguel Delaney published a long polemic headlined "The fight for football's soul: How corporate greed and political apathy poisoned the English game". Delaney outlined, and railed against, the failure of state authorities to protect football clubs from untrammelled market forces: "How have they just been left open to the highest bidder, whoever that may be?" He points to a historic lack of interest from government in clubs as cultural and social institutions, as well as the failure of various forms of protective legislation, most notably the fit and proper persons test, which was designed to protect clubs from 'improper' owners and has proved laughably inadequate for the task.

Almost a year earlier, in September 2018, Jon Henderson published *When Footballers Were Skint: A Journey in Search of the Soul of Football*, which promised to take readers back to a time "Long before perma-tanned football agents and TV mega-rights ushered in the age of the multimillionaire player," when "legends such as Tom Finney and Stanley Matthews shared a bond of borderline penury with the huge crowds they entertained", and "players and fans would even sometimes be next-door neighbours in a street of working-class terraced houses". Two years before that, Neil Lennon (then managing Hibs) railed against Rotherham's decision to sack Alan Stubbs as manager after 13 games, despite having given him a three-year contract.

> It's losing its soul. For me, the reason to be in football was to play, to compete and get the glory and improve. That's what managers want to do but they're not giving them the time because money is the be all and end all. [...] I think it just needs a lot more patience.

Three years before Stubbs was let go, in July 2013, Gordon Taylor (then chief executive of the players' union) reflected on a visit to former Middlesbrough and Burnley right-back Gary Parkinson, who had suffered a stroke earlier that year.

> I saw the way his family had looked after him and the way football responded. It is about that. [...] I don't want people thinking it's all about money, where money is the only gauge of success. I think the game is in danger of losing its soul because I think about youngsters playing football, having the facilities, aspiring to be like heroes and we're not working hard enough on that.

The common thread uniting all of the above is, of course, money, or perhaps more accurately the intertwining of capitalism and football. The sale of social institutions to the highest bidder, regardless of their distance from, interest in, or care towards the club itself as anything beyond an investment; a twitchy lack of patience in the boardroom; the swelling paycheques of the elite players and their subsequent departure from their club's community into distant celebrity enclaves: these are some of the signature features of the football industry as it is practiced in the early years of the 21st century.

October 2011 was a particularly fruitful moment for the soul conversation. Alex Clark and Danny Kelly — the former supports Arsenal; the latter Tottenham — published a conversation in the *Guardian* under the headline "Has football lost its soul?". Kelly averred that football has "sold its soul for Mammon":

> The rapacious search for what the sporting bodies call 'maximised revenue' has turned those of us who used to

be spectators into 'customers' and has led to the endless background disputes that currently curdle football. Lifelong Arsenal fans bemoan ticket prices at the Emirates; Chelsea attempts to strong-arm its supporters into accepting a move away from their traditional heartland; Tottenham and West Ham engage in a shameless, undignified scramble for a stadium funded by the tax-payer; across the border, Celtic and Rangers are permanently locked out of the love-in. Football is the ultimate child of Thatcherism. It has gathered together great riches while alienating its core audience.

That same month, Rob Smyth and Georgina Turner published *Jumpers for Goalposts: How Football Sold Its Soul*.[48] Unlike some previous entrants in the canon, which treat the soul of football as something self-evidently good and equally self-evidently missing, Smyth and Turner begin by attempting to define what the soul is, even as they say it is "virtually impossible to grasp [football's soul] tightly enough to hold it still, yet lightly enough to appreciate its contours and colours in your hands". Cleverly, they outsource the responsibility to a Soul of Football XI, trusting that the shape of the thing will become apparent when we imagine the playing patterns of Dave Mackay and John Charles, Danny Blanchflower and

---

[48] In fact, if we are to locate the soul of football anywhere, the best place to look might be the subtitles of books about football. As well as the Henderson book already mentioned, other post-millennium examples include David Conn's *The Beautiful Game?: Searching for the Soul of Football* (2005), *Sing When You're Winning: Football Fans, Terrace Songs and a Search for the Soul of Soccer* by Colin Irwin (2006), *Theatre of Silence: The Lost Soul of Football* by Matthew Bazell (2011), *Up Pohnpei: A Quest to Reclaim the Soul of Football by Leading the World's Ultimate Underdogs to Glory* by Paul Watson (2012), *Is the Baw Burst?: A Long-suffering Supporter's Search for the Soul of Scottish Football* by Iain Hyslop (also 2012), *Another Bloody Saturday: A Journey to the Heart and Soul of Football by Mat Guy* (2015), and most recently Tim Hartley's *The World at Your Feet: One Man's Search for the Soul of the Beautiful Game*, published in 2021. Note that nearly all these souls are things to be searched for, high and low, near and far. As much as anything else, this is a Grail quest.

Sócrates, with Lionel Messi and Stanley Matthews on the wings and César Luis Menotti puffing away on the touchline. Here the soul is something created by players: a motley concatenation of artists and mavericks, agitators and dreamers, the brave and the bold and the interestingly brilliant, though one wonders if Matt Le Tissier's recent turn into Covid-19 conspiracising might force Menotti to make a change up front.[49]

But if the soul itself remains still partially obscured, Smyth and Turner are confident that the moment of sale can be identified.

> History generally demands staging posts, and for that purpose, 1992 is football's *annus ridiculus*. It's the year that the European Cup became the Champions League, and the year that British football — with which most of this book is concerned — was made an indecent proposal, and accepted; we're not far off the point where Sky is actually paying £1 million a night.

That indecent proposal was, of course, the foundation of the Premier League. That the top division of English football would wish to break away from the Football League and go about the business of making its own money had been discussed before, and so did not come as a surprise to anybody, although many were shocked by the FA's ready acquiescence. And that this might result in the loss of football's soul was anticipated even as the deal was being made. In March 1992, Neil Harman's column in the *Daily Mail* was headlined "Bad day as soccer sells its soul to the screen".[50] He announced "the game stands accused today of an act of betrayal, selling its soul for 304 million pieces of television silver. [...] Sold down the river to Rupert Murdoch's henchmen."

---

[49] To take just one example from what has been a dispiriting year for Le Tissier, in March 2021 he strongly implied — on Twitter, naturally — that the death of John Magufuli, president of Tanzania and voluble opponent of vaccinations, could be traced back to the Bill & Melinda Gates Foundation.

[50] A 'soccer', in the wild in the UK, in the 1990s! Although perhaps headline writers have the excuse of needing to save space.

Murdoch's position as owner of a rival tabloid might not be incidental here, and of course the *Mail* itself has since adjusted, orienting its online presence around the new reality of hyper-rich celebrity football with breathless scoops such as "Manchester United star Memphis Depay spotted on supermarket shopping spree for toilet paper, water and Capri Sun".

Hardman turned to the New Testament for his analogy, but the really tempting parallel comes at the very beginning of the Old. English football, tempted by a whisper from Rupert Murdoch, gave in and ate from the Tree of Knowledge of Greater Profit, and so it Fell. Exiled from paradise, the game has wandered deeper into the wilderness, its soul besmirched beyond recognition by that original sin. Even Sky Sports' irritating habit of dating statistics from the formation of the Premier League, not the Football League, has the effect of rendering everything before 1992 vaguely mysterious, as if football back then was in some fundamental sense unformed and ahistoric. This, of course, helps the Sky Sports project: there is no better way to assert ownership of something than to declare everything that has gone before as part of a different age, now passed and fading.

It is tempting to conceptualise this as football somehow coming under attack from capitalism, which would make the proclaimed loss of the soul a lament, or perhaps a rallying cry, depending on how optimistic the author is feeling. But as Tom Williams has pointed out for *New Socialist*, capitalism has always been in football just as football has, since its coalescence, always been in capitalism: "Capitalism organises football, but not in conditions of its choosing. And football doesn't simply allow itself to be organised — it resists. Contemporary football is constituted by struggle and contradiction." Perhaps it is better, then, to think of all these various post-1992 symptoms of the lost soul as *consequences* of this struggle, rather than defeats for 'the game' and victories for the invading forces. Indeed, in some cases they represent problems for capitalism, or at least for those capitalists that might want to own a football club and extract a profit from it: swelling player wages and agents' fees make that a profoundly tricky project. As Williams notes, the Super League made less sense as a cash grab — though it would certainly have been that — and more as a response to a perceived crisis of profitability: more "a question of desperation and weakness than greed, or perhaps desperation assuming the form of greed". Even before the pandemic and its associated economic hit, many of the game's superclubs were laden with debt, and it is probably not a coincidence that the first two English clubs to change their minds were Chelsea and Manchester City, both run on the kindly benefactor model: Jack Walker SuperHyperPlus. Whatever Roman Abramovich and the United Arab Emirates want from their football clubs, they don't need the money.

In any case, the severance of the Premier League from the Football League in 1992 did not emerge unanticipated and context-free. The breakaway sits logically (if dramatically) in the lineage of the various changes to football since professionalisation, changes that have altered both the character of the sport and the character of the business of the sport, generally by permitting a greater flow of money through the game and, thus, a stretching of hierarchies and the concentration of power at the top of the pyramid. Though, again, not always serving the particular interests of the owners. The maximum wage for players was lifted in 1961, and the old retain-and-transfer system that gave clubs control over their players' movements followed shortly afterwards. In the 1980s the game abandoned gate-sharing between home and away teams and the four percent gate levy shared across each division, and began to direct 50% of centrally negotiated television money to the top division. And in 1983, the FA permitted Tottenham to float on the stock market, in the process overturning their own Rule 34, which had previously limited football club ownership to private limited companies and prevented directors from taking a wage. If this was a fall, it came in stages; a stumble and a trip from grace.

And while 1992 may mark the intensification of this search for a lost soul, it was not the beginning. We can trace the soul, and its loss or its losing, back through English football history. In 1982, former England captain Alan Ball announced his retirement from the game at the age of 37.[51] *The Daily Mirror* recorded his relief at the decision — "There's nothing left for me any more" — and his lament at the state of the game he was leaving:

Football no longer belongs to the man in the street, the kids, or the players. There's no passion left. It's just a job now. It's lost its soul. At one stage the prospect of not playing anymore terrified me. Now I'm glad I'm getting out. There are no rascals around any more. I've always been the first to spend my money, first to buy a drink and the first to enjoy myself. It's getting a bit lonely.

We can already see the shape of many of the objections that people will go on to raise about the Premier League, here in the early demo stage. Players removed from ordinary fans; the game professionalised to an undesirable degree; the fun somehow sucked from the whole business. There is, too, in that word 'rascals', a nod towards a disappearing dressing-room culture, to a simpler time when men were men and lads were lads and boys were allowed to be boys.

Moving further back, it appears that the *Times*' journalists of the 1970s were mostly concerned with the soul as discovered in the presence or missed in the absence of beautiful football. In a preview of the 1975 FA Cup Final — headlined "Fine balance of a romantic match" — an unbylined writer praises Fulham for breaking their habit of inconsistency; a habit that sprang, apparently, from their players' tendency towards both "brilliance" and "bathos". But despite this newfound reliability, it is "to their credit [that] Fulham have never wanted to become a soulless football factory. Craven Cottage industry accommodates aesthetic as well as functional qualities."

A year earlier, in 1974, Scotland played Zaire in the World Cup. In a sprawling match report, the *Times*' man in Dortmund compares the Zaire team, with their "musical, tongue-twisting names", to leopards — the team's nickname — but also lions, snakes, tropical

---

[51] This interview was given in October 1982 — Ball ended up playing until the end of the 1983/84 season.

birds and, somehow, "ants in a half-destroyed anthill". They were "an eye-opener. They have a dance for everything. They dance for the moon under the moon." And, crucially, Zaire's football "was far less boring than much of the scientific, cynical and soulless football that this World Cup may well produce ... This was as fresh as a summer breeze on a lovely summer night."

Even without the metaphor-safari, this characterisation of Zaire as *un*scientific, *un*cynical — they were the only African side at the tournament — is at best uncomfortably patronising, at worst honkingly colonial. Apparently football writing still hadn't shaken free of the old racist trope of the noble savage, naively happy in a state of pristine pre-civilisation. All this serves to reinforce the Edenic metaphor: humanity unfallen and uncorrupted, without history or rationality. And what are science and cynicism if not the application of knowledge, the very thing for which Eve exchanged eternal bliss. Here, Zaire's football is held to have a soul precisely *because* it is uncorrupted.[52]

Staying with the *Times*, drifting back another couple of decades, this comes from the report of Moscow Dynamo's 1-0 defeat of Sunderland, in November 1955.

> The scientists say that sound is never lost. Somewhere the roars of the Roman mob still reverberate. Somewhere the voice of the north-east on this night perhaps will still survive.

---

[52] This image of Zaire as footballing naïfs was sealed in the western imagination when, as they prepared to defend a free-kick in their last group game against Brazil, Mwepu Ilunga ran from the defensive wall before the whistle had gone and kicked the ball away. He was booked, the watching world laughed at the silly African who didn't know the rules, and the clip has been a staple of football's banter-industrial complex ever since. However, Mwepu later explained that Zaire's players were preoccupied: after losing 9-0 to Yugoslavia in their second game, they had been visited by the Presidential guards of Marshal Mobutu, who informed the squad that they would not be permitted to return home if they lost their next game by more than four goals. Already 3-0 down and in the 85th minute, Mwepu's dash from the wall looks, in hindsight, less like a hilarious error and more like a canny, desperate, entirely rational piece of time-wasting.

But it now quite failed to breathe any life and fire into their heroes … in attack, which is the life and soul of football, there came only a melancholy spark. Now and then there was promise of some inspired play from Shackleton, but truly the only magic that persisted was the magic of the floodlights against the velvet night.

These pieces all share a common thread: the soul of football is to be found within attacking endeavour and attractive football. As well as their names, Zaire's players are praised for playing in an attacking 4-2-4 formation — "unusual these days" — and for passing the ball around their scientifically rigid opponents. Fulham are saluted for ensuring that their players grow up to produce beauty as well as end product; for retaining a place for the craftsman in a world of industrialised production. Sunderland, for their part, cannot manage anything of the sort, and so are soulless, lifeless, lightless, entirely without magic.

Moving back further, between the wars, we find the concern about football's soul has moved from the pitch to the stands. In 1926, a referee named Peter Craigmyle stood up in front of a crowd at Edinburgh's YMCA Hall to deliver an address entitled "Has Football lost its soul?" According to The *Scotsman*'s record of the evening, Craigmyle was arguing against those suggesting that it had. These people — Craigmyle claims an opposition of thousands; it is unclear how many were made of straw — were arguing that football had been robbed of its soul by the appearance of interested, club-specific fans; by the emergence of partisanship in the game's followers. "All this noise and din was not good for the game".

Craigmyle punches back in spirited fashion.

Without noise you could not have football. The people went there to encourage, to sympathise, and to applaud. Football was watched by hundreds of thousands of people, and it was not losing its soul. There was not one game that had such a terrific hold on the masses of Great Britain as this game of football, the best game and the cleanest game. The Lord Provost, the Town Councillors, the artisan, the labourer, and the message boy — they all went to see it. It was a democratic game.

And, most delightfully, he offers up an ancestor of later arguments. For what is "There were many people who went to watch only one team, and football could not be football if that were not the case" if not, *avant la lettre*: football without fans is nothing.

We can go back further still. In *Beastly Fury*, a history of the early days of English football, Richard Saunders recounts the disappointment of 'Pa' Jackson at the Football Association's decision to waive residency requirements for professionals, so allowing anybody from anywhere to be paid by any club: "From that moment, he believed, football lost its soul." And going right back to the source, at the meeting in London in 1863 that resulted in the codification of The Laws of the Game, a number of clubs refused to sign up to the Football Association's grand project on the grounds that they could not conceive of football if it did not permit hacking — that is, kicking an opponent in the shins in an attempt to reclaim the ball. Famously, F.W. Campbell of Blackheath FC proclaimed that, if hacking were outlawed, then "you will do away with all the courage and pluck of the game, and I will be bound to bring over a lot of Frenchmen who would beat you with a week's practice". Football was supposed to be about pain, endurance, and physical fortitude in the face of moustachioed men charging in just below the knee, and what greater expression of a loss of soul could there be, for an Englishman, than the prospect of being beaten by the French.[53]

I have lifted the conceit of this chapter wholesale from Raymond Williams' *The Country and the City*, in which the critic and novelist traces a sentiment that feels immediate and of the moment — in his case, the idea that the rural way of life has been destroyed by the rise of urban Britain — back through literature and through time, finding echoes and expressions of that same sentiment as he goes. He acknowledges that this is, in part, the apparently banal habit of appealing to the good old days, but notes too that each of the "successive Old Englands" exists on its own terms, in a particular

---

[53]   Although France are currently ahead of England by two World Cups to one, and by two European Championships to nil, so the prediction holds.

relation to the moment from which it is looked back towards. "Nostalgia," he writes, "is universal and persistent." Ultimately he identifies "a continual pattern of retrospective regret, going back to that golden age or that most potent of all idealised places, the Garden of Eden."

The underlying meaning behind the assertion of Craigmyle's opponents, of the *Times*'s match report writers, of Alan Ball, and of the widespread sentiment occasioned by the Premier League and then amplified by the Super League is the same: the thing that makes the game what it is has gone, or is going. But the particulars are of their moment. Campbell wanted to preserve the healthy violence he believed fundamental to the sport; Jackson the delicate compromise between professionalism and amateurism that had been negotiated only a few years before. Craigmyle's intellectual opponents were mourning the passage of that same Corinthian spirit, only now among the fans, who could no longer enjoy the game for the sake of the game but only for the tyranny of the result. The *Times*' journalists were lamenting the state of the game as it was played: the decline of attacking endeavour, the rise of scientific cynicism. Ball was consumed with despair at the passing of the rascals, squeezed out of the dressing room by the logics of professionalism. And the list of objections to the hyper-accelerated post-1992 money fight is, as we have seen, enough to fill several books, but almost all can be understood as emerging in one way or another from football's mutative interrelationship with capitalism.

Williams notes that "a memory of childhood can be said persuasively to have some permanent significance", and perhaps, on an individual level, this questing attitude is inherent to any interest — passion; obsession — acquired while young. A fan is cursed to always be looking back over their shoulder at their receding childhood, convinced that the gates of Eden are visible in the golden haze of youth; a haze that mystifies even as it promises. Convinced, too, that a path can be cut back to that place. I am not suggesting that this means resistance or complaint at the state of football now is in some sense futile: on the contrary, fighting for the soul of something beloved seems among the more worthy ways of spending one's time. Whenever one's time might come. But it only seems natural that this postlapsarian malaise has led to calls to get the game back to Eden.

The loose collection of fans that fall under the banner of 'Against Modern Football' is often described as a movement, yet in truth it is something more inchoate. Perhaps 'AMF' is better understood as a sentiment, variously and differently expressed; one that has been easily transferred from country to country, shared and adapted across local contexts. Having emerged from the ultra culture of Germany and Italy, it has spread across continental Europe and beyond, manifesting in blog posts, banners, tweets, fanzines, YouTube videos, more tweets, podcasts, stickers, tattoos, manifestos, and almost any other medium of expression available to football fans. Much of the sentiment is inarguably positive: few would disagree that, for example, lower ticket prices and greater fan involvement with clubs could only be for the better. But it is far from uncomplicated. Here's Leander Schaerlaeckens, writing in *Vice*:

> Ridding itself of all that hatred, of the skinheads and flares and generally threatening mood in roiling cauldrons, has served the sport's bottom line very well. In the 1980s it would have been unthinkable to bring your family to an English stadium. Today, you can do so safely, sitting in the midst of respectable businessmen. [...] Families and businessmen and tourists tend to leave more money behind. This, ultimately, is the central conflict that gave rise to Against Modern Football. When gains were made to further commercialization and overall safety, something of the sport's smell and feel was lost for its original demographic base.

As noted previously, many new and newish stadiums, both within England and beyond, have been identified as soulless, ahistoric, unatmospheric: as lacking the affective power that makes going to football what it is, or made it what it was. AMF, then, is interested in restoring that feeling; yet by that interest it lays itself open to the charge that, wittingly or unwittingly, it is advocating a return to a time that many found unpleasant, plenty found exclusionary, and a few found actively dangerous. At an individual level, English football is still not an entirely unthreatening place, but it's a lot more welcoming than it used to be for anybody that doesn't present as cis, white, straight, and male. That has less to do with the sudden appearance of respectable businessmen in the stands and more to do with broader social shifts and hard organisational work from within fanbases and communities — indeed, the idea that bigotry is inversely related to social class is not just grotesque but wildly inaccurate, as anybody that's spent any time with the English middle classes will be able to attest. But the good old days were rarely good for everybody. The fanzine *STAND*, first published in the UK in 2012, was originally called *Stand: Against Modern Football*, until editor Bill Biss dropped the subtitle after receiving "a lot of criticism for somehow wanting a return to the dark days of hooliganism and racism, even though we've always said we're not about that".

Yet even taking those who travel under AMF in good faith in this regard, the sentiment hangs heavy with nostalgia and, in its implication that the *true* practice of football support has been lost and must be reclaimed, a kind of authento-revanchism. Imbuing past models of support with properness elides all sorts of awkward questions, and fails to interrogate how these spaces came to be and who was able and permitted to occupy them. A sport that is gatekept by price is a shabby and diminished thing; so, too, a game that is off-limits or uncomfortable for anybody on the grounds of their gender, race, sexuality, or neurotypicality. I noted earlier that football grounds had become more welcoming places and, while this is true in general, it is still not reliably true in the specific; indeed, a number of journalists have suggested that, pre-pandemic, live football was getting worse in this regard, mirrored by an appalling recent explosion in racist and misogynistic abuse online. The sight of England fans treating London to the world's largest stag do ahead of the final of Euro 2020 was a reminder that football can be a deeply unpleasant, even invasive presence. And even where overt bigotry and harassment is hidden away, many matchgoing fans have stories of more subtle exclusions. How long have you been coming to the match? Are you here with your boyfriend? She fell over! She fell over!

I am acutely aware that my overarching suggestion in this book, that a football club's identity is made in large and crucial part by its fans, might easily be employed in the search for some authentic model of support rooted in the past. I should make clear, then, that just because any given club's identity has emerged from its fans acting as fans, this does not amount to an assertion that such spaces were perfect as they were, or that it would be a worthwhile project to recreate them faithfully down to the last Stone Island patch. There are many powerful and wholly legitimate reasons why any given fan might not have been present in any given space, by choice or by circumstance, and the fact that this may have excluded them from some part of the club-making process must not be read as implying that it should. Must not be read, in fact, as anything other than a failure and a shame.

A regular banner at Dulwich Hamlet proclaims its owners to be 'For Future Football', a position that, while perhaps less consoling in its promises, has always seemed to me more clear-eyed and hopeful.[54] Future football, then, might be oriented around these two principles: maximal radical inclusivity, and maximal radical democracy. Clubs that are open to anyone; clubs that are accountable to the ensuing everyone. Fan ownership of one form or another is a start here, but only a start. This is not the place and I am not the writer to lay out any detailed plans, but I would assert that if the fans make the club, then only by ensuring that any fan that wants to be a part of that process, can be, will we end up with clubs that are truly grounded in, drawn from, and made by their communities. If football without fans is nothing, that goes for any given fan just as surely as it goes for all.

---

[54] Unfortunately, the acronym is FFF, which in a footballing context has already been taken by the French Football Federation, and has, according to the Urban Dictionary, all kinds of exciting alternative meanings beyond the sport.

Chapter Ten:
Structures of feeling

Having happily hacked apart the idea of a soul as it relates to a football club, we should probably conclude by trying to pull it all together again. The first thing to re-emphasise is that very few of my respondents or other sources seem to believe their clubs to be actually ensouled, in any of the various senses that a religious believer might consider a person, human or otherwise. Rather, the soul is deployed in all cases as a metaphor.[55] It is a particularly interesting metaphor because it is remarkably flexible (as we have seen) and it is ultimately vague (what is a soul?), and yet at the same time it is extremely clear. As the poet and essayist Kathleen Jaime puts it: "Such a thing may not exist, but we want it, and we know what we mean when we talk about it."

So when we talk about a football club having a soul, we are saying that there is life here, there is vitality and significance and character and perhaps even beauty of a sort. And we also mystify

---

[55] The idea that an animist soul might be metaphorical is a controversial one within anthropology. Rane Willerslev has charged that construing animist beliefs as metaphors reduces animism to "a 'false epistemology', resulting from the [alleged] inability of indigenous peoples to distinguish metaphor from reality": "the anthropologist accepts the indigenous statements about the existence of nonhuman persons only by adding an 'as if' to their accounts". However, for our purposes, as far as I can tell the metaphorical nature of this soul is already presumed by my interlocutors: this is not a theological claim, despite the theological language, and so the "as if" comes already inserted.

the conversation. To assert a soul is to assert that any discussion about a football club must attend to something beyond the mundane. The power and utility of the soul-metaphor comes from this mystification, a productive tension between knowing what we mean but not knowing it precisely. When we use a soul metaphorically we insist on a fundamental layer of mystery even as we delineate space and function: we make an inexplicability explicit. 'The soul' points towards the thing, and it points towards the thing's value, and it points towards the thing's unknowability. So when we summon up the idea of a soul and speak it into the world to signify some aspect or other of a football club, we are saying of that aspect: *I do not quite know what this is, and I am not entirely sure how it works, and I don't know how I would even prove that it exists; but I know that it does exist, I know that it is important, and I know that without it the club will in some sense die.*

Why might a football fan feel this way? What is it about supporting a football club that might provoke such mysticism? It would be unkind to call it a cliché, but a lot of how-I-became-a-fan-of-my-club stories begin in much the same way: with the feeling of the thing. I've already mentioned a couple earlier in this book, including Dave Roberts' liniment-and-cigarette-infused trip to Bromley and Iain Macintosh's cussing collective. Here are few more examples, from an article published on the BBC website in 2015, 'Memories from your first football match'.

My first game was at Dundee United in the UEFA Cup. I remember a sea of orange and the smell of burger and onions.

Shouting, singing, smell of liniment, sledging the opposition goalie on run-up to goal kicks.

Freezing to death at Burnden Park aged 12 on my own. Sat next to an old man who did not speak a word to me, at the start of the second half he emerged with two cups of Bovril and handed me one. Never seen him before or since and still love Bovril.

Something similar happens to Bobby Robson's imagined child: they go up the steps, they see the pitch, and they fall in love. The common thread here is the child, the soon-to-be-fan, being taken into a new and unusual place and being confronted with something that is different. Different sights, different smells, different sounds; people behaving differently to the norm. It is, above all, a sensory moment, one that first discombobulates and then reconfigures. In goes a child; out comes a fan. And then, next week: in goes a fan, out comes a fan, on and on. Here's the 'Greasy Chip Butty Song', as sung by fans of Sheffield United and a few other clubs:

> You fill up my senses
> Like a gallon of Magnet
> Like a packet of Woodbines
> Like a good pinch of snuff
> Like a night out in Sheffield
> Like a greasy chip butty
> Like Sheffield United
> Come thrill me again

Football support, at its heart, is a thing that is felt. And the feelings of supporting a football club are manifold and operate on a variety of scales. There are feelings intimately bound up with the matchday experience, starting with the immediate sensorial affect of the ground in the moment: the smells and the sounds and the rain blatting in your face and running down your neck. There is tension, appalling tension, as the game passes and the result gets closer and the seconds stretch into minutes and the minutes into hours. There are the rushes of emotion that come with a goal, or a great save, or an appalling refereeing injustice; there is, perhaps elevated above all other football feelings, the great tangle of limbs that comes in an away end after a particularly significant goal. There is, too, the inverse, the heavy gnawing boredom that comes during dull games when nothing is happening and nothing seems likely to happen. Football is often boring, and to be a football fan often means confronting and negotiating that boredom.

But football is also funny, at times overwhelmingly so. I can think of no comparable source of emergent humour. At a fundamental level, football multiplies the universal comic appeal of 'people falling over' by the universal comic appeal of 'people taking something far more seriously than they probably should', and puts that all in front of an audience that is allowed to shout things while being equally guilty of the second part. I remember very little of my first game watching Dulwich Hamlet, in September 2010, partly because I am very bad at watching football as football and partly because the game wasn't very good. But I vividly remember central defender Francis Duku calling for a high dropping ball, setting himself for the header, realising at the last second he'd slightly misjudged the flight, and *kneeing* the thing. It flew back up into the air along more or less the same path it had come from, nearly taking his head off in the process, and I laughed and laughed and quietly fell in love. Perhaps you had to be there.

There are, too, the larger feelings that come with a club that is *yours*: that can be provoked in you by *your* team, by *your* players. These beautiful people, these incompetent clowns, these beautiful incompetent clowns. Joy and pride one week, frustration, bafflement, even contempt the next. There is the feeling of commonality, of belonging, that comes from sharing some or all of the above with your friends, your family, your wider family of strangers, with the crowd as a whole. There is the joy of representing your community, of demonstrating who you are and where you are from: "the feeling of belonging, the pride in your city." And there is, as discussed in chapter six, the overarching sense of participation in some grand historical continuity, of being part of and witness to a club that extends through time before you and after you as well.

It is important that football can always promise collective joy; it is perhaps equally important that it doesn't always deliver, that there is always an unrealised potentiality. And, of course, every football fan knows that even the moments when it does deliver are already shifting from the present to the past. Don't take me home. Please don't take me home. Joe Kennedy has suggested that football is ultimately structured around anxiety: "Any sense of completion which the game affords is shadowed by the awareness that this sense is illusory and contingent and, indeed, the primary satisfaction offered by football is inescapably coloured with morbidity and perversity, a pleasure taken in the anticipation of approaching unpleasure."

And there is one more feeling we should add to the list above, which has been one of the themes of this book: the sense of a club's fans that a club's owners and administrators do not care about them. A perceived distance, even opposition: them against us; executive box against terrace. As noted previously, this is felt in different strengths at different clubs, generally does not reach the point of full and formal secession, and is often framed — particularly at the higher end of the Premier League — less as an existential question of good governance and more as a problem of investment and consequent competitiveness. But I return again to that survey, to the FSF's finding that for more than two-thirds of football fans, it is a known feeling. I would guess that most of the rest have felt it at some point in the past, even if they were lucky enough to be happy at the moment they encountered the question. And I think it is fair to characterise it as a feeling: a lot of what goes on at a football club is opaque and so the fans' response is less a considered assessment of known information, more a question of tension and disquiet, trust or the lack of it.

I am sure that the list of football-feelings above is not exhaustive; I'm not sure any list could encompass everything and everyone. But it will do as a starting point, and I think it's fair to say that for the majority of fans that centre their football support on a particular club, most of their football-feelings are bound up within that club. The moment-to-moment feelings are given their particular character by the performance of the team and the character of the ground; the broader and deeper feelings are determined by the apprehension of history, identity, commonalities past and present. The processing of and response to the former determines the latter; the latter provides context and reference for the former. And, of course, football clubs themselves have attempted to capture these feelings: plenty of

English clubs, big and small, emphasise their deep historical roots in their marketing materials, and the roar of the crowd has been commodified just as surely as the game itself, even as the Premier League's clubs scramble to find some way to keep the promise of that roar within a heavily commercialised game. As the game has got quieter, the advertorial insistence on the importance of the noise of the game has got louder. It is notable, too, that clubs often look to play up the *distinctiveness* of these feelings, as though being, say, a Liverpool fan — 'This Means More' — simply feels *better* than being any other fan, in an important way that doesn't just mean winning quite a lot.

To return to Raymond Williams, it is here that his idea of a 'structure of feeling' may be of some use. It is a slippery idea, one that I happily admit to finding as elusive as I do interesting. A structure of feeling is not something as formally codified as a world-view or an ideology, nor is it just a way of thinking about emotions and felt responses in themselves, through the immediate feelings. Rather, per Williams, we are thinking about "social experiences in solution": sociality, the peopleness of people with people, dissolved into something larger, held within it but not consumed by it. There is a pleasing liquidity about this idea of a solution. This is not a rigid structure that confines, but a fluid one that shifts, shapes and reshapes.

Perhaps we might say that every club has its own particular structure of feeling. The club extends into the physical world as a football ground and into the sporting world as a football team, but these extensions are peopled with and followed by the fans, who make the club by standing around the pitch and by caring about and reacting to what happens on it, with each other, week by week and season by season. All that sociality, all those different but connected subjectivities, dissolve into the club and so, over the years, each club is *felt* into its particular and characteristic self. In *Marxism and Literature*, Williams describes structures of feeling as "not feelings against thought, but thought as felt and feeling as thought: practical consciousness of a present kind, in a living relationship to continuity".

To my mind that works beautifully to evoke the kind of thinking-unthinking state of being a football fan: intellectually engaged with the club but also emotionally subjected to it, watching the game but also being worked upon by the game, and how those notionally distinct positions operate as one integrated and dynamic whole.

Perhaps we might say, too, that when we speak of the soul of a club we mean just this structure of feeling, this social solution, in its best aspect. As it could be, as it should be, as it is in the good moments. And when we speak of soullessness, we mean a club that does not *feel* right, for one reason or another, be it a miserable ground or a distant owner, a lack of hope or a lack of direction. The old cliché has it that team spirit is an illusion glimpsed in the aftermath of victory; perhaps we might say that a club's soul, whether present to be protected or absent to be rediscovered, is a metaphor used to denote the shared social happiness of happy clubs and the communal misery of the miserable.

There is one other consequence of imaging a soul, one other sense in which 'we know what we mean'. A soul, at least in the western imaginary, is one half of a familiar conceptual duality: it requires a body just as a body aches for a soul, and both relate to each other in a reciprocal hierarchy that is immediately comprehensible even if it is stubbornly hard to delineate precisely. This is baked into the very language of football, right there in the Latin root: *corpus*. The executives sit in the corporate boxes, exercising their corporate functions, and just as they constitute the body so by implication, and as Bobby Robson knew, they cannot constitute the soul. Instead, the fans occupy this physical extension and, through their persistent occupation and by simply being fans, fill it with resonant and ordinary-extraordinary incorporeality: character, anima, soul, vivacity, buzz, energy, atmosphere, *life*. The metaphor of the soul serves to emphasise that which is fungible set against that which is fundamental. What is left behind when the solution is boiled away.

Mark up!

One of the more interesting long-term consequences of Wimbledon's move is that the process of founding the new club created within English football a network of knowledge-sharing and collaboration. AFC Wimbledon were not the first fan-led breakaway club — that would be Enfield Town, founded in 2001 after a number of fans concluded that Enfield FC's owners had no desire to return the club to Enfield — but their high profile as FA Cup winners and fairytale monsters, and the vast media coverage that ensued, effectively made the personalities involved into national figures of a sort.[56] Accordingly, various people associated with the founding of AFC have gone on to provide advice, assistance and inspiration to other clubs in similar situations. In his book *Red Rebels*, founding member of FC United and former *Red Issue* editor John-Paul O'Neill describes Kris Stewart telling an early meeting of the rebels that "as and when any FC United team took the pitch, no matter what had gone before them, that would feel like *your* club" (original emphasis). Then, after the rebels don't quite get as many pledges as they were hoping, O'Neill heads to the pub in low spirits.

> The feeling that supporters could make a difference had evaporated. The reality was nothing could be done. [...] Outside in the beer garden, Kris Stewart asked what was up. 'The backing's not there, so that's the end of that,' I said. Stewart looked a bit puzzled. 'So what? Do you think you could still pull it off?' he asked. 'Yeah. Of course we could,' I replied. 'Well, there you go.' He knew what he was doing. The challenge had been set.

The key line there is: "He knew what he was doing". The establishment of AFC Wimbledon has not just been a success on

---

[56]   Enfield Town play at the Queen Elizabeth II Stadium in north London, which boasts a Grade II listed art deco clubhouse: the overall effect is that of a cruise ship, chimneys trimmed away, almost entirely buried by the side of a football pitch. Do note however that the stadium is multi-sport, and while admiring the pavilion take care — here I very nearly speak from experience — not to fall into the long jump pit.

its own terms. It has been a powerful statement: a refutation of the idea that Wimbledon in Wimbledon was not in the wider interests of football, and a reminder that 'the wider interests of football' is a contested idea. And it has also been a practical demonstration of the organisational capacity that football fans possess. In the full gaze of the national press and the wider footballing community, the founders of the breakaway proved that fans were capable of founding a football club; they have since proved that fans are capable of running one all the way up to professionalism, all while getting a ground built. Further, and arguably much more importantly in the wider scheme of things, they demonstrated that a club could be established around what the fans held to be the point of a football club. In this sense 'the soul of a club' isn't just a question of metaphysical handwaving: it is a thing around which the fans can organise. Once a soul has been identified, even where it is not named as such, then it can be defended from those who might threaten it. It can be asserted, in the face of those who might diminish it. And ultimately, in the most extreme circumstances, it can be taken somewhere better, somewhere kinder, somewhere safer. We might even detect a pattern here: when the questions around a football club's future sharpen and become existential, the language mystifies to meet them. Consider Kris Stewart's rejection of life in Milton Keynes as another form of death: a non-corporeal death, zombification, death despite the still-living body. Consider, too, the founders of AFC giving a foundation date of 1889 to the FA: an assertion of continuity, of an unbroken lineage passed from body to body. Consider the title of Niall Couper's excellent multi-vocal history of the club: *The Spirit of Wimbledon*. This slide into the mystical comes when it is not just the corporeal stuff of a football club that requires attention and protection, but the animating force.

Williams advances the idea of a structure of feeling as a way of problematising hegemony, that terrible invisible oppression that insists things are as they are because they must be; that they could not have been any other way. "The pressures and limits of what can be seen as a specific economic, political, and cultural system," he writes, "seem to most of us the pressures and limits of common sense". A structure of feeling is one way of conceiving of a way of living and thinking within hegemony that contains the possibility of disrupting or displacing what is hegemonic; as such, hegemony can never be totalising.

It is both tempting and encouraging to think of AFC Wimbledon and the other fan-owned clubs, whether rebel or phoenix, as amounting to a rejection of the ludicrous, money-driven, and — yes — soulless circus that is much of professional football. And it is absolutely correct to do so: there is always succour to be drawn from the story of a group of people who, having been told they both couldn't and shouldn't do something, decide to ignore all that and just get on with it anyway. In *Punk Football*, his history of the rise of fan ownership in English football, Jim Keoghan identifies AFC Wimbledon as the "poster boys" of a DIY movement, which sees "ordinary fans eschewing the established system and deciding that there is nothing stopping them from getting together to run the clubs". There is much good truth in that.

We should be careful, however, not to overstate the case. AFC certainly amounts to a disruption of the way in which professional football clubs have typically been constituted — a state of affairs that seemed common sense but turned out to be contingent and changeable — but they are still, in a broader sense, part of the same overarching system. The sporting and economic logics of the pyramid still apply, even if fan-run clubs can generally be expected to take fewer risks with the club's future in pursuit of a quick path up the divisions. They stand as an example of how a better way might be found within the knot of football and capitalism, but they do not unpick it.

This is not a criticism. The point of AFC Wimbledon was not to stage a utopian experiment within the pyramid and so bring the pyramid crumbling down: it was to ensure that everybody in and around Wimbledon that wanted to watch their football club could do so. The disruption that has followed has come through this struggle, and the way in which it has forced English football to confront and interrogate its own presumptions. If AFC do amount to a small step towards a better game in general, and I firmly believe that they do, it is for the most part through this sense of expanded possibility supported by practical example: that fans can organise around their idea of a club, whatever that might be and however they might conceive of it, and carry it forward on their own terms. In *The Football Man*, Arthur Hopcraft wrote that the game "was not so much an opiate of the people as a flag run up against the gaffer bolting his gates and the landlord armed with his bailiffs." Here, the locked gates were those of the club itself, the landlord the owners, yet the flag and the people carried the day.

I will conclude by reiterating that by my evidence, and by anecdotal experience, not all and not even most football fans conceive of their club as having a soul of one kind or another. Some find the idea laughable, others desperately pretentious. But I would suggest that most if not all would know what 'the soul of a club' referred to, and most would recognise the dangers that come with 'soullessness', even if they wouldn't choose to put it in those terms. Following a football club, loving a football club, is a mysterious thing to do. It has a value that exceeds the transactional and approaches the numinous; and just as well, since if we were to break it down into a transaction — money and time for football — it is often poor value. That is precisely why we must not. The totality of the feelings of being a supporter, and the place those structured feelings come to occupy in a life, is testament to the fact that there is something about any club — about every club in its own way — that transcends the tangible and the immediately comprehensible. Call it a soul, call it nothing at all: for every club it can be seen, however darkly, and in moments of crisis it emerges with great presence. The thing that is most important about the thing. The thing that makes the thing, the thing.

Afterword:
In these unprecedented times

I began the work that would become this book towards the end of 2017. If you'd asked me then what I thought of a possible Super League, a breakaway of all the biggest European clubs, I would have said it was a stupid idea. I would then have added, in a slightly irritating tone of voice: ah, but that's the point. Actually breaking away would be messy, expensive and potentially legally disastrous, but the *threat* of a breakaway is a useful tool for the big clubs in their ongoing mission to secure a larger share of football's money. Give us more, or we'll leave. Thanks. Give us more, or we'll leave. Thanks again. And that's why it will never happen. It isn't supposed to.

I didn't see Covid-19 coming either, but I'll let myself off there.

Football, the national game and the national distraction, was enlisted early in the British response to Covid-19. The professional and semi-professional game shut down completely in March 2020, but the Premier League and Championship were back by June and finished by the end of July. Leagues One and Two concluded their season on an average-points-per-game basis and then held playoffs behind closed doors, and the National League did the same. Then, after a highly truncated break, the new season began for the top four divisions in mid-September. Football's return felt hasty, and its continuation through the end of 2020 amid rising cases and another national lockdown felt, at times, grossly inappropriate. But it kept going, driven by the suggestion — not least from several government ministers — that the return of football would serve as a reassuring beacon of normality in strange times.

Project Restart was many things, including gratefully received on the whole. But it was not in any sense normal. Premier League games went free to air and some even appeared on the BBC. The 3 o'clock Saturday afternoon broadcasting blackout was ended, as every top flight game was moved into its own slot. Away teams got changed in car parks, in Portakabins and T-huts. Players celebrated at a distance, at least for the first few games. Ball boys were gone: sanitised spare balls sat on plinths around the edge of the pitch. And the strangest abnormality of all: no fans.

The most immediate effect of the closure of all stands and terraces was to render every football fan in the country a television fan: there was no other option, beyond not watching at all. All those circuits, those patterns of habit, paused. Broken. If a football club — or at least what is important about football clubs, however we might choose to understand that — is a thing that is made and continually remade by fans being fans together, then we have just been through a year and more of practical exile. The simple business of being in a crowd was understood to be reckless and dangerous, and it was also illegal. Accordingly, this process of club-making was at that moment in a holding pattern. If it was happening, it was happening at a distance: in online spaces, in support bubbles, in the group chat. In memory and reminiscence and the shared sense of hope that things could one day begin again.

Meanwhile, there was the television. Moving every Premier League game to television meant that fans lucky enough to support a team in the top flight could still follow their team, but the blanket coverage combined with the lockdown meant that football fatigue became a common complaint. Actual fatigue diminished the spectacle, too: without a proper preseason and with a compressed schedule, the players were visibly knackered halfway through the 2020/21 season and running on fumes by the end.

The television was strange as well. The very first games broadcast after football's return were sent out into the world with just the sound of the game being played in an empty stadium. This was odd yet familiar: it turns out the sounds of a high-level football game without a crowd are essentially similar to any game played without a crowd at any level. Chatter between teammates, on-field organisers barking orders, goalkeepers keeping their defence in line, yelps of pain at sharp tackles and so on.[57] Perhaps the most estranging factor was the aural effect of large but empty stadiums, which produced for television a metallic echo that sounded almost exactly like a leisure centre swimming pool.

But this demystification of the great and the good was not allowed to last for long. The solution to this not-quite-a-problem was fake crowd noise, which quickly became the standard across all television channels and later on radio (though some TV channels did provide the option to switch back to just the stadium noise). Fake crowd noise, largely sourced from video games, provided one useful service to the casual television viewer: if you weren't paying too much attention, it sounded just like there was an ordinary game of football on in the background.[58]

The problem came when paying attention. When actually watching a game, the sounds immediately become uncanny, or perhaps more precisely *weird*, as finessed by Mark Fisher: the weird is that which does not belong with the familiar and cannot be reconciled with it. Fisher suggests that the form "most appropriate" to the weird is montage, the "conjoining of two or more things which do not belong together," and that is precisely what the fake

---

[57] Thin consolation, but at times it was extremely entertaining to hear the world's elite footballers chirupping away like human beings. Without the absence of the Emirates crowd, we might never have heard Arsenal's Rob Holding complain to the referee, after fouling Adama Traoré: "He's built like a brick shithouse, how's he gone down like that?"

[58] There is an interesting recursive loop here, in that the best-selling FIFA series of video games has, over the years, increasingly attempted to recreate not the experience of playing football but the experience of watching football on the television. As video game critic Steve Burns put it: "The entire presentation aims for nothing less than an accurate rendering of the match-day experience, as seen on your TV."

crowd noise offered us: an unlovely splicing of sounds that sat not-quite-right with each other and not-quite-right against the images. What worked passably well as background noise became janky and awkward when brought into focus. It was good but not perfect, it was almost right and thus jarringly wrong. You could hear — you could not help but hear — the soundtrack lurching from file to file, from background_4 to buildup_3 to excitement_6, then quickly on to goal_1 and cheer_7, and then, once it became clear that the shot had passed just outside the post, a whiplash back to disappointment_3 and then oh_good_a_corner_2. I am sure that I am doing a disservice to a complex and admirable technical achievement, but for any game in which close attention was paid to the action, this Frankensteined soundtrack was a constant reminder of the incorrectness of things. Until the fans returned, Charlton Athletic were stuck playing at the Uncanny Valley.[59]

This could be funny, as when a bad tackle flew in and your imagination summoned up the image of a technician sitting at a soundboard, furiously hammering a large red button marked 'BOOOO'. But it could also be bleak, particularly for those fans who would, under normal circumstances, be present in the stadium and making their own noises. My friend, the writer, filmmaker and Norwich City fan Juliet Jacques, described watching games broadcast from an empty Carrow Road — seeing the bright tarpaulin stretched over her seat, hearing the fake crowd noise fail to accurately reflect the frustrations of a poor team's crowd — as "the most unbearable feeling I've ever experienced as a football fan ... total alienation". And the players hated the empty stadiums too. Writing in the *Guardian*, Burnley captain Ben Mee noted that he and many other players had "struggled to get the same rush of adrenaline before a match."

---

[59]   I prefer weird to uncanny for the broader point, although that wouldn't work for the joke. But the alternative and perhaps more precise translation of Freud's *unheimlich* — 'unhomely' — is particularly resonant when it comes to all these empty football stadiums. It is the presence of the fans that 'homes' the stadium; it is their absence that renders it strange.

Everyone wants fans back and we will all appreciate being able to see one another again, having full stadiums and being able to get that buzz back. I cannot wait to walk out into a packed ground and have everyone enjoy their football.

The pandemic isn't over as I write this afterword, just before the 2021/22 season, but fans have begun to return to England's football stadiums. The 2021 FA Cup final played out in front of 10,000 supporters and, while it is nice to believe that Leicester were directly inspired to victory by the presence of their fans, we can certainly say that the fans and the sound of fans immeasurably improved the spectacle. Fake crowd noise never really cracked the way in which the sound of a football crowd is layered with nervous tension and often, in moments of high excitement, becomes significantly more complex than simple cheering. Apparently there was no appropriate sound for '5,000 desperately relieved supporters loudly mocking their former left-back for being an inch offside while also making hooting noises in praise of a video review system that they mostly actually hate and in addition all shouting "COME ON!" at their own team, or their friends, or themselves, or just generally in the direction of the heavens, in the vague hope that God hasn't got money on Chelsea'.

When fans finally return in full numbers and voice, it will be a poignant moment, not least because not all fans will have made it through the interruption. Some circuits will not be renewed. Most English clubs mark a minute's silence at the end of each season for fans that have passed in the course of the campaign, but it was notable at the end of 2020/21 that many clubs went to a far greater effort than usual, pulling together photo montages and presenting names of those lost in the pandemic. Grief is an ever-present if sometimes quiet part of following any football club, as over the years the unseen faces and unheard voices gather, present absences laced through the crowd.

As for the clubs themselves, up and down the pyramid the future is uncertain. All have lost money, and what support has been available has been poorly communicated and haphazardly administered. Speaking in September 2020 when it was still unclear whether the National League season would begin at all, Maidenhead United chairman Peter Griffin predicted that without further support from the government "everyone will be out of a job and club after club will go bankrupt. If there isn't further help now, all the money that has been pumped into football clubs to help them keep going will just be wasted money. It will be for nothing." In the end, the National League season did begin in October, but it was cancelled in February in the middle of a row over this extra support, which had been promised as grants but ended up being offered as loans. Some clubs, reluctant to take on the debt, failed to fulfil their fixtures and were issued fines even as the whole competition was mothballed again.

Up at the very top of the pyramid, where everybody else saw a crisis, the big boys saw an opportunity. We got a future echo of the Super League in October 2020 when John W. Henry, owner of Liverpool, brought Project Big Picture to the nation. The wide-ranging proposals included some obviously good ideas (more revenue shared by the Premier League, caps on away ticket prices, safe standing), and plenty more that was at least interesting (reorganisation of the calendar, relegation playoffs), though the headline move was the concentration of the power to make future changes to the organisation of English football into the hands of just six clubs, the biggest and the richest, including of course Liverpool. This made the entire project look like a grubby power grab, and it was unanimously rejected. So in April 2021, Liverpool came back with 11 friends and made a much larger, much grander, much grubbier power grab.

To say the Super League went down badly would be to push understatement well beyond its capacities. Perhaps nothing has ever gone down quite so unanimously badly. Even Radio 4's Today programme, an institution so pathologically committed to the he-said-she-said model of journalistic balance that they would happily both-sides a Möbius strip, couldn't find anybody to come on and give the idea a good word. Online, the derision reached an almost carnivalesque pitch, reminiscent of that time Samir Nasri visited the Drip Doctors or that time we all found out about David Cameron and the pig.[60] Offline, everybody with access to a microphone or a television camera lined up to register their disappointment. No, their disdain. No, their *disgust*. Players, pundits, politicians, administrators from other clubs, administrators from the leagues, UEFA, then FIFA, and of course almost every fan organisation in England. The whole thing lasted barely 48 hours, as first Manchester City and Chelsea pulled out, then the rest of the English teams, and then finally, Atlético Madrid and the two teams from Milan.

Afterwards, with only Real Madrid, Barcelona and Juventus keeping the dream alive, it was common to hear people wondering "What were they expecting? How were they so unprepared?" But that's not quite right. The breakaway clubs were prepared for one very specific form of opposition: at the moment the Super League was announced, they made submissions to a court in Madrid designed to preempt and prevent any legal challenge to their right to form a new league. That was the opposition they anticipated and were prepared to face down. The rest was miscalculation, not obliviousness. According to gossip email *Popbitch*, Liverpool's owners consulted three separate PR firms about the move, and all assured the club that the reaction from the fans would be positive.

Just as the Premier League clubs used the financial requirements of stadium improvements to justify their breakaway, so too the Super League clubs sought to present their move as being a question of necessity in expensive circumstances, not avarice or desperation. The pandemic had been expensive: this is how the super clubs needed to pay for it. As noted in chapter nine, even a passing familiarity with football finance rendered this position highly implausible, and you didn't even need that to perceive its fundamental tastelessness. But I do wonder how much the timing played into the response. Partly I mean this in a broad sense: had England's football fans

---

[60] Perhaps the only moments in human history when it was better to be on Twitter than not.

been reminded, by the reduction of football into a television show, just how unfulfilling football as a television show can be? The plan suggested the Champions League on steroids, and the branding — just 'Super League' — strongly hinted at a future of games on tour, tapping into target markets around the world. I don't quite want to suggest that the country was seized by some plague-inspired spasm of Corinthian ideals, but if there's a good time to talk about completely shattering the fabric of the world's most popular sport, it's probably not when everybody's desperate for the return of some kind of normality.

And partly I mean this question of timing very precisely. The announcement came late on April 18. The following day, Liverpool played away at Leeds United, and were greeted by 700 fans who chased the team bus down the road. The day after that, more than a thousand Chelsea fans gathered outside Stamford Bridge: they blockaded the team bus, club legend Petr Čech disembarked to plead with them, and then the whole scene erupted in cheering as news filtered through that Chelsea were pulling out of the scheme. A few days later fans gathered outside Arsenal's and Tottenham's grounds, and on April 23, ahead of their home game against Liverpool, protesting Manchester United fans stormed Old Trafford, paraded across the pitch, and forced a postponement. "We Say When You Play" read one banner. Football without fans' permission is nothing.

England's roadmap for exiting lockdown wasn't scheduled to begin until early May, but in late April there was a general sense of optimism about restrictions lifting soon. Much of the international situation remained deeply worrying, and the Delta variant hadn't yet emerged as a broad concern, but there was positive news about the UK's vaccination programme and infection rates were falling across the country. Also the days were getting longer and the weather was getting better. As such, I'm guessing that there were plenty of football fans looking for any excuse to get together, let off flares, sing songs, and generally exist as a collective for the first time in more than a year. If there's a good time to talk about completely shattering the fabric of the country's most popular sport, it's probably not when people are feeling a little bit of hope for the first time in a while but are also still bored out of their minds.

As I was writing and worrying about this book, one particular fear kept coming back: what if this is all just a little bit too late? What if this model of a football club that I'm talking about, that Bobby Robson was talking about, that so many of my survey respondents were talking about ... what if it's already gone? Lost to the market logics of the Premier League and the cynicism that trickles down, lost to the ossified competitive structure, lost to the tightly controlled and highly securitised matchday experience, lost between the rocks of celebrity and the whirlpool of tourism. What if these circuits were vestigial traces, evacuated of all energy and distinct only in the shapes left behind — what if football has no room left for these reflexive, creative, communal love stories? What if this whole exercise in not-quite-anthropology was, in fact, an exercise in not-quite-archaeology?

The near-instant, near-universal response to the Super League didn't quite allay these fears, but it did suggest that there are limits to what football fans, even those that might notionally benefit from the idea, will allow to be done to their game. Just for a moment the ratchet slipped, and football seemed to spin freely in the breeze, there for whoever could take it.

What actually happens remains to be seen. As regards competitions, UEFA agreed on reforms to the Champions League that won't go as far as the Super League in securing the eternal presence of the biggest teams, but will still reserve places for teams based on their historical record: better, but some distance from good. The UK government has promised a wide-ranging consultation on the future of the game and has set up a panel to conduct a 'fan-led' review. The panel's interim findings, published in August 2021, called for an independent regulator for English football; broad financial reforms with particular regard to the flow of money between the divisions. They also suggested that "heritage assets", including home grounds, location, name, badge and kit colours, be protected by a "golden share" and a right of veto, to be held by a democratically-elected body of fans. Joining the call for an independent regulator, perhaps an Ofside to go along with media's Ofcom and education's Ofsted, is a collective of ex-players and high profile pundits led by Gary Neville and Gary Lineker. And AFC Wimbledon and a few other EFL clubs have signed up to an initiative called Fair Game, which seeks to reorient football club ownership around four principles: community, independent regulation, integrity and sustainability.

It seems obvious that English football will be a political football for some time to come. You'd never describe the current UK prime minister, Boris Johnson, as being in any sense #AMF — indeed, one of the advantages of his brand of Wodehousian malignity is that he doesn't even have to pretend to be into football. But at least in its public statements, this particular mutation of British Conservatism is a long way from Thatcher's unconcealed contempt for football fans. Johnson was quickly and publicly vocal in his opposition to the Super League, and it's easy to see how English football and in particular the Premier League — an English success story on the international stage! Up yours, Europe! — might find a place in the bumptiously isolationist imaginary of post-Brexit Toryism.[61] Though the panicked reversal of the government position on booing England players for taking the knee, and the obvious contempt those players have for the government's clunking anti-wokeness crusade, suggests that this may not be an entirely straightforward project.

But for a moment, there was power in football that belonged to the fans, and there was solidarity operating between those fans, and I suspect that even if the initial post-Super League settlement is underwhelming or flawed, the memory and the promise of that power and solidarity will sustain hope for some time.

---

[61]   It has been reported that contrary to Johnson's strong and immediate opposition to the Super League, the clubs in question had been given the nod from No.10. According to the Mirror's source, the matter was discussed with Johnson's chief of staff just days before the announcement, and "Boris doesn't know much about football so he said it was a great idea." So if nothing else, let's hope everybody involved has learned important lessons about who can and cannot be trusted.

There has already been some practical impact: the Big Six clubs have been relieved of their positions on Premier League committees, Chelsea and Tottenham have both offered to involve fans at boardroom level, and there is renewed energy in the ongoing campaign against the Glazer family's ownership of Manchester United. As well as protests, fans are now targeting United's commercial partners, and a £200m deal to sponsor United's training kit for the next 10 years has recently fallen through under pressure from the fans. Perhaps rattled, the Glazers are responding: Joel Glazer made an appearance at a United fans forum in June 2021, promising investment in the team and in Old Trafford, and also the creation of a Fan Advisory Board and a Fan Share Scheme.

And there have been other moments of hope, even through the pandemic. For the first time in a generation, fans of a football club in Wimbledon got to watch their team play a game at a ground called Plough Lane. Lockdown restrictions meant this historic occasion was a post-season friendly with limited attendance, but the process of re-establishment has begun, and the return that everybody important said was impossible and undesirable has been completed.

In the brief period between lockdowns, when such things were permitted, Juliet and I went to a few non-league games around London. One of them, a trip to watch Balham host Hassocks in the extra preliminary qualifying round of the FA Cup, delivered everything that a footballing drifter could ask for. First a bit of needle, then a late and moderately controversial equaliser, and finally a penalty shootout.

To get to the end where the penalties were being taken, we had to squeeze behind the dugouts and then under some scaffolding, being careful to avoid a few over-enthusiastic brambles. But we were well-rewarded: the penalties were decent, and the goalkeepers were putting on their best show, diving and sprawling and ruefully slapping their gloves together. All for the crowd. All 130 of us. Seven of the first eight penalties were more or less unsaveable, with the exception of Balham's second, which was hit hard but not quite straight enough. Hassocks' keeper, diving away to one corner, was able to stick his leg back against his momentum and deflect it away.

So to Hassocks' last kick, again unsaveable. As his teammates observed the traditional form and ran to congratulate their goalkeeper, the goalscorer peeled away to the side of the pitch opposite the dugouts and the brambles. In the damp autumn night, in the buttery yellow light of the floodlights, he approached the near-empty grandstand and dipped into a full and perfect kneeslide. In my memory, he travels perhaps 20 yards; I will accept that this is likely an exaggeration. I will, too, accept that he probably knew one of the few people in the stands. But from where we were standing with the drizzle in our eyes, he appeared to be delivering this celebration, this provocation, to a few hundred plastic seats. To a vacant space where fans should have been. It seemed a dedication, almost a votive act, a candle lit in honour of a promise maintained. Even without you, he seemed to say, as he pumped his fists towards the empty seats and screamed into the empty air. Even without you, that was for you.